Mutual sexual fulfillment is the desire ⌐⌐⌐⌐ often seems illusive. It may seem strange to Christian ears that God has that same desire for your marriage. In *God, Sex, and Your Marriage*, Dr. Juli Slattery clarifies the power of letting God into the marital bedroom. Understanding God's perspective has the potential of greatly enhancing your sexual relationship.

GARY CHAPMAN
Author of *The 5 Love Languages*

This is a MUST READ for every married couple. And even singles. Juli brings a wisdom and insight into God's design for sexuality that will deepen your understanding of God's dream for married sex, but also of God Himself. Her teaching on "yada" is worth the whole book. Get it. Read it. Apply it. And share this book with others because these truths are needed now more than ever.

DAVE & ANN WILSON
Cohosts of *FamilyLife Today*

T. S. Eliot once observed that we must first know what something is for if we are ever to know what to do with it. The same is true of sexual intimacy in marriage, which makes *God, Sex, and Your Marriage* by Juli Slattery such an important book. Beyond the dos and don'ts, Juli offers the big picture of why God created sex in the first place.

JOHN AND SARAH STONESTREET

If there are parts of your sex life that are too painful to even think about, let alone talk about, this book is ESSENTIAL reading. In the arena of Christian sex help, Juli brings a unique and much-needed perspective, helping us understand how the pursuit of true sexual intimacy begins not in the bedroom but in the throne room. Eminently practical and relatable, this book makes my heart sing when

I think about the hope and healing that this message will bring to couples who feel stuck and demoralized.

ROSIE MAKINNEY
Director, Fight For Love Ministries

God, Sex, and Your Marriage is an excellent and theologically sound resource that incorporates spirituality and sexuality. Colossians 3:17 says, "And whatever you do, in word or deed, do everything in the name of the Lord Jesus" (ESV). Dr. Slattery teaches how we can enjoy sex in the name of Jesus and grow in our relationship with Him through God's gift of sex. This book will help you grow in your walk with Christ and in your enjoyment of your spouse.

BRAD AND MARILYN RHOADS
Cofounders of Grace Marriage

GOD
SEX
YOUR *and*
MARRIAGE

DR. JULI
SLATTERY

MOODY PUBLISHERS
CHICAGO

Edited by Amanda Cleary Eastep
Interior design: Ragont Design
Cover design: Erik M. Peterson
Cover illustration of puzzle copyright © 2020 by Bohdan Kotoshchuk/iStock (1204289471). All rights reserved.
Author photo: Kate Thomas

Library of Congress Cataloging-in-Publication Data

Names: Slattery, Julianna, 1969- author.
Title: God, sex, and your marriage / Dr. Juli Slattery.
Description: Chicago : Moody Publishers, 2022. | Includes bibliographical references. | Summary: "Many Christian books talk about sexual issues within broader works on marriage, but few resources comprehensively and biblically guide couples specifically on sexual intimacy. God, Sex, and Your Marriage challenges the common assumptions couples have about sexuality and presents the richer biblical narrative of sex as a metaphor of God's covenant love. Dr. Juli Slattery applies that biblical framework to the practical challenges in sexual intimacy. Godly sexuality extends far beyond sexual purity and calls us to sexual integrity. God invites every couple to view their sexual relationship, including their greatest struggles, as an avenue to learn about the nature of His covenant love. It's God's desire to make us more like Himself, and sex within marriage is often a powerful training ground for godly character. That desire gives purpose and context to addressing pornography, healing from past wounds, sexual incompatibility, pursuing pleasure together, and forgiveness"-- Provided by publisher.
Identifiers: LCCN 2022002751 (print) | LCCN 2022002752 (ebook) | ISBN 9780802429018 | ISBN 9780802474001 (ebook)
Subjects: LCSH: Sex--Religious aspects--Christianity. | Marriage--Religious aspects--Christianity. | BISAC: RELIGION / Christian Living / Love & Marriage | RELIGION / Christian Living / Men's Interests
Classification: LCC BT708 .S539 2022 (print) | LCC BT708 (ebook) | DDC 261.8/35--dc23/eng/20220302
LC record available at https://lccn.loc.gov/2022002751
LC ebook record available at https://lccn.loc.gov/2022002752

Originally delivered by fleets of horse-drawn wagons, the affordable paperbacks from D. L. Moody's publishing house resourced the church and served everyday people. Now, after more than 125 years of publishing and ministry, Moody Publishers' mission remains the same—even if our delivery systems have changed a bit. For more information on other books (and resources) created from a biblical perspective, go to www.moodypublishers.com or write to:

Moody Publishers
820 N. LaSalle Boulevard
Chicago, IL 60610

3 5 7 9 10 8 6 4 2

Printed in the United States of America

*This book is dedicated to my brothers and sisters in Christ—
some who have labored before me and some
who now work beside me in reclaiming God's design for sex.
The field is ripe for the harvest but the laborers are few. May the God
who gives endurance and encouragement grant us harmony with one
another in Christ Jesus, so that with one mind and one voice we may
glorify the God and Father of our Lord Jesus Christ (Rom. 15:5–6).*

Contents

Introduction

Why God Cares about Your Sex Life (and You Should Too)

"What do you do for work?"

It's a question I usually dread. How do I tell the person sitting next to me on an airplane or my husband's coworker that I run an organization that "reclaims God's design for sexuality"? After all, the person was just trying to make light conversation. As strangers, neither of us have a desire to wade into conversations about anything related to sex.

But, that's my job. Although I don't like explaining it to a stranger, I am genuinely passionate about the work to which God has called me.

Don't get me wrong. I don't enjoy talking about pornography, the cultural clash of biblical sexuality and social justice, sexual trauma, or really any specific sexual issue. These are very sensitive and difficult topics that represent a tsunami of pain for most people. But I also recognize that we need help navigating sex from a biblical perspective. While the larger culture speaks endlessly about sex, those who represent God have stayed relatively quiet.

To be honest, I needed help too. My husband, Mike, and I know what it feels like to struggle with God's "gift" of sex in marriage. I've felt the shame of having questions that I didn't know how to ask. Even as a clinical psychologist and marriage counselor, I secretly struggled for over fifteen years of my marriage with a conflictual and difficult sex life, not knowing where I could turn for help. I just assumed that sex was always going to be a struggle. Some couples enjoy sex, but I believed that just wasn't going to happen for us. During the most discouraging years, I wondered why people would refer to sex as a gift at all.

Maybe you're in the same situation. Instead of unity, sex creates conflict. Rather than bringing pleasure, sex represents pain. While sex was intended to foster the intimacy of being deeply known, it actually evokes a deep shame that makes you want to hide from each other.

If this describes you, I want you to know that you're normal. Practically every couple I talk to describes sex, for one reason or another, as a difficult area of their marriage. But don't confuse normal with healthy. Just consider that the normal American is overweight, overstimulated, exhausted, and lonely. In a similar vein, the normal marriage has a storage room full of baggage related to sexual frustration and conflict. While it is very common for a married couple to have significant conflict in their sex life, remember that what's normal can often be described as dysfunctional.

> **Practically every couple I talk to describes sex, for one reason or another, as a difficult area of their marriage. But don't confuse normal with healthy.**

What's normal in marriage is some level of frustration and resentment about why sex is unfulfilling. It's normal for both the husband

and wife to enter marriage with baggage, like a history of porn use or past sexual partners. Unfortunately, it is normal for both men and women to have experienced the devastation of sexual trauma or exploitation. From what I've observed, most Christian couples who find themselves running into these normal barriers to intimacy just give up. Some eventually leave their marriage to find a more compatible soul mate, and many others endure through years of simply existing as roommates.

Far too many couples attempt to use tools to improve sex in their marriage without a fundamental understanding of what they are supposed to be working toward.

What you read in this book may be a different approach to sexuality than you have ever heard before. It's frankly a book that I wish someone had given Mike and me as we began our marriage. You're not going to find diagrams of anatomy, recommended sexual positions, or basic information to improve your sex life. I don't want to replicate the wonderful resources already available that walk through the physical and emotional fundamentals of sex. Two that I would recommend: *A Celebration of Sex* by Doug Rosenau and *The Gift of Sex* by Cliff and Joyce Penner. In this book, we are going to take a look at the foundation of why sex matters in your marriage and what to do in response. Far too many couples attempt to use tools to improve sex in their marriage without a fundamental understanding of what they are supposed to be working toward.

In this book, you will learn two important truths. First of all, sex will never be a neutral issue in your marriage. By its very nature, sexual intimacy was created to draw you together in body, soul, and spirit as "one flesh." This powerful gift, when used wisely, will create a magnificent bond between a husband and wife. But that same power can be turned against you and become the source of pain and division in your marriage.

You may be surprised to discover that while you and your spouse have significant sexual problems in your marriage, sex can be a glue forging your hearts together. Sex unites you not simply when it is fun and satisfying, but when you journey together through disappointment and discouragement.

Secondly, sex will never be a neutral issue in your relationship with God. In this book, you will read about how sexuality was created to be a divine metaphor, teaching us about the nature of God's covenant love. Our sexuality should actually be drawing us into greater intimacy with God! However, for most people (including Christians), sex is a barrier to knowing God. It represents the shame of moral failure or pain that we believe a loving God should have eliminated from our lives. For many Christians, God and sex is a very confusing combination.

I care about your sex life because God cares about your sex life. Yes, you read that right. God cares about your sex life. He knows your secret thoughts and frustrations. He doesn't leave the room when you and your spouse get naked or even if you look at porn. While this reality might make you feel somewhat awkward, God's presence with you is not to condemn you but to invite you into healing.

I remember the day when God made it clear that He was calling me to start a ministry focused on sexuality. I was on my knees, praying and fasting, and this passage from Isaiah flooded my mind:

> The Spirit of the Sovereign LORD is on me,
>   because the LORD has anointed me
>   to proclaim good news to the poor.
> He has sent me to bind up the brokenhearted,
>   to proclaim freedom for the captives
>   and release from darkness for the prisoners,

to proclaim the year of the LORD's favor
and the day of vengeance of our God,
to comfort all who mourn,
and provide for those who grieve in Zion—
to bestow on them a crown of beauty
instead of ashes,
the oil of joy
instead of mourning,
and a garment of praise
instead of a spirit of despair.
They will be called oaks of righteousness,
a planting of the LORD
for the display of his splendor. (Isa. 61:1–3)

This Old Testament prophecy spoke of the coming of Jesus and the work He would do in humanity. That day in July of 2011, I saw that it also applied to the work Jesus does in redeeming our sexual brokenness. God brings good news! He wants to bind up our broken hearts and give us freedom from our shame and the darkness of our sin. He comforts us who mourn and replaces our despair with praise. His redemption in all areas of your life, including your sexuality, displays God's glory and splendor!

WHAT TO EXPECT

Whenever my husband confronts a challenge that involves hard work, he says, "It's like eating broccoli and doing push-ups." When we have a compelling vision for health and wholeness, we make everyday choices to work toward that goal. There are parts of this book that may feel like "eating broccoli or doing push-ups." I'm inviting you to think about sex in a way that may seem foreign to you. Whether you have a good sex life in your marriage or you are really struggling,

God wants to reveal some truths that may transform how you view sex and intimacy. As you read, this book will prompt you to have some uncomfortable conversations with your spouse and with the Lord. But remember, sex isn't just about the hard work. You choose to engage in the work because you desire the greater good of what God designed sexual intimacy to be within your marriage.

This book is divided into two sections. Part 1, Foundations of a Great Sex Life, will help you identify ways your understanding of sexuality sets you up for frustration and disappointment, and you will learn how to think about sex from God's perspective. Part 2, Pillars of a Great Sex Life, will teach you the four key characteristics of a thriving sexual journey in your marriage. The final chapter will give you some next steps to consider. The book also contains a study guide for each chapter to be used for personal study, conversations as a couple and small group discussion.

I'm excited that you've decided to take this challenge! I know God will meet you in each step you take toward His amazing design for sexual intimacy.

Part 1

FOUNDATIONS OF A GREAT SEX LIFE

Chapter 1

Knowing Your Backstory

When our three sons were little, one of their favorite toys was LEGO bricks. I spent practically every Christmas morning for over a decade helping them build castles, spaceships, and villages. The worst thing about a building block set is realizing that somewhere along the way, you got a step wrong. Misplacing just one piece in the building process will distort the whole project. Often my sons and I would find ourselves carefully deconstructing what we had worked so hard to build in order to discover where we went wrong in the building process.

Your sex life is a lot like this. You can tell that something isn't right. Maybe you can even pinpoint a specific problem like past sexual trauma, the impact of porn, body parts that won't cooperate, or a huge difference in sexual appetites. But underneath those problems is, most likely, a faulty foundation upon which you've been building your sexual relationship.

When I talk with married couples, they often want solutions to the obvious problems they are experiencing in sex. A wife asks, "I've never enjoyed sex. How do I get into it when I'm exhausted all the time?" Her husband wants to know, "How can I get my wife to be more adventurous in bed?" As a couple, they want help recovering from infidelity or navigating body image issues. These are important and practical questions. But before dealing with the practical aspects of sex in marriage, couples need to do some deconstructing to ensure that they are building from the right foundation.

To put it bluntly, I have the sneaking suspicion that you may be working with a wrong understanding of the purpose of sex in your marriage. Why? Because I certainly was. I was raised in a wonderful Christian family, attended solid churches and Christian schools, and earned three advanced degrees in psychology, giving me practically every advantage in my early marriage. Even so, it has only been within the past decade that I've learned a framework for sex that has revolutionized how I approach this topic in every area of life, including my marriage.

No matter what challenge you and your spouse are dealing with in your sex life, your framework for how you understand the gift of sex is absolutely essential for addressing the real-life questions you are asking.

WHAT'S YOUR BACKSTORY?

Imagine that you are binge-watching a Netflix series. Your spouse plops down next to you in the middle of episode five and begins peppering you with questions. Why did they shoot that guy? Is that the love interest? Is she a spy? Pretty frustrating, right? You probably respond with the obvious, "You have to watch the first four episodes to understand what's going on in this one."

Backstory is everything. It paints the picture for how we understand and interpret the events that are happening right now. Have you ever considered that your sex life has a backstory? And your spouse's sex life has one as well. These backstories include what has happened between the two of you and also what you experienced before you ever met.

Your sexual backstory is not just the things that happened to you as a teenager or young adult, but how those experiences shaped *how you think about sex.* You don't come to your marriage bed with a blank slate. You come with expectations, fears, secrets, shame, and an unspoken understanding of what "good sex" should look like. Take Sam and Emma as an example.

Emma was raised in a conservative religious home. Her parents rarely talked about sex other than "check-ins" to make sure she didn't go too far with her high school boyfriend. Her church youth group once did a series on God and sex, from which she walked away learning that it was her responsibility not to make the guys in her life "stumble."

When she went to university, even the Christian guys she hung out with engaged in casual sex with female friends. Sex was a form of recreation and was certainly expected in any dating relationship. Although Emma was more conservative than most of her friends, she was sexually active with a few of the guys she dated.

Two years out of college, Emma and Sam met through mutual friends. It didn't take long for Sam to share his view of sex and why it was important for them to set physical boundaries in their relationship. Sam had a history of porn use that began when he was eleven. In college, Sam got connected to some guys through a Christian ministry that introduced him to God. As part of his discipleship journey, Sam began addressing porn use in his life. He regularly met with a group of guys who asked him to be honest about whether or not he was looking at porn. Sam admitted to a "stumbling journey" toward purity. Some months were good and some were bad.

Bottom line, Sam couldn't wait to get married so he would finally have an approved outlet for his sexual desires and fantasies. The couple was married within a year of first meeting. Family and friends celebrated with them and waved goodbye as they set off for their new life together.

Fast-forward several years. Emma and Sam have navigated through many of the challenges of early marriage, but sex continues to be a rough spot. They experienced the clumsiness of newlywed sex, but the real problems began a few months later. Sam shut down. He found that he had no desire to be sexual with his wife. When she flirted with him, he changed the subject. Although he was married to a beautiful, passionate woman, Sam found himself reverting back to porn and masturbation, and he couldn't figure out why.

Emma went into a downward spiral of sadness and insecurity. She wondered if this might be God's punishment for sleeping around in college. She felt completely rejected by Sam. "When we were dating, he couldn't wait to have sex with me. Now, he doesn't even look at me when I'm naked. What's wrong with me? Why am I not enough for him?" Add a few children and years of unspoken shame and frustration, and this couple doesn't know how to begin addressing the issues that sex represents.

Or consider the backstories of Amy and Jim. Amy was raised by a single mom who had a series of live-in boyfriends. When Amy was ten, her mom's boyfriend began making sexual comments toward her and eventually began molesting Amy. The abuse continued for several months until Amy's mom discovered what was happening. Although her mom kicked the guy out of the house, she never spoke to Amy about the abuse. Without any guidance and filled with sexual shame, Amy followed her mom's example of going from guy to guy until she met Jim.

Jim brought his own pain into their marriage. Although he wasn't sexually abused, he grew up in a family that was emotionally distant. The only way Jim understood closeness and intimacy was to be sexual with his wife. Not long into their marriage, Jim became very frustrated when Amy began avoiding sex. Jim continually made sexual advances, only to be shot down again and once again. Every time Jim initiated sex, Amy froze. When they did have sex, she felt used and violated.

As a Christian couple, Amy and Jim knew sex was supposed to be a gift from God. They couldn't understand why God would give them a gift that represented so much pain and disappointment.

Out of the tangled experiences of their backstory, sexuality for both of these couples has come to represent some strange blend of blessing from God, shame from the past, and unmet expectations.

If I were meeting with couples like these, they would want to know how to get on the "same page sexually." They would want to understand why one of them avoids sex and why they are so hurt and disappointed with something they were told to look forward to. Instead of answering these questions, I might begin by asking them questions like, "Why do you think God created you as a sexual person? What do you think it means to be sexually whole or sexually broken?"

> **You can't *do* sex right in your marriage until you *think about* sex correctly in your marriage.**

Friend, you and your spouse cannot solve the problem of sex until you have the right perspective of what it's supposed to look like in the first place. You can't *do* sex right in your marriage until you *think about* sex correctly in your marriage. And most likely, your backstory has muddled your perspective of what it means to be a sexual person.

Whether or not you are aware of it, sex was rich with meaning before you ever said "I do." Even the avoidance of sex has purpose. Sex is not just two bodies connecting, but involves the complex interchange of everything sex has come to mean to both you and your spouse. Your backstories live beneath the symptoms of mismatched sexual desire, a request for "kinky" sex, and the longing for what you can't quite grasp.

We use templates or narratives to try to make sense of why sex is so difficult, how to solve our problems, and whether or not it's even worth trying anymore. Most Christians view sex through a combination of both the secular culture's perspective of sexuality and a simplistic version of religious teaching on the topic.

THE CULTURE'S STORY OF SEX

The culture's story of sex is all about experiencing personal pleasure. Sex is supposed to be great! To be a truly happy person, you must be with someone who is consistently meeting your romantic and sexual needs. If you and your spouse are fighting about sex, you may simply be sexually incompatible.

Scholar Blaise Pascal who lived more than three hundred years ago noted that, "There is a God-shaped vacuum in the heart of each man which cannot be satisfied by any created thing but only by God the Creator, made known through Jesus Christ."[1] When we run away from God, we must fill that void with something. For many, the answer is romantic love and sexual fulfillment. While sex in our world has been cheapened, at the same time it has been elevated to represent our identity, our value, and our happiness.

Rather than viewing sex as something that God has created for His glory, our culture tells us that sex is a morally neutral aspect of what it means to be human. Our greatest good is to be sexually fulfilled and satisfied. In a 2016 study, the Barna Group concluded:

The move among the greater U.S. population—most evidently among younger generations—is a de-linking of marriage and sex. Sex has become less a function of procreation or an expression of intimacy and more of a personal experience. To have sex is increasingly seen as a pleasurable and important element in the journey toward self-fulfillment.[2]

Based on the culture's story of sex, you should explore your fantasies and desires because this is a crucial part of finding your true self. Anyone (including God) who hinders your sexual expression and fulfillment is morally wrong because they are keeping you from happiness. Don't stay in an unfulfilling marriage. Don't get married unless you try it out with cohabitation. Don't let anyone tell you who you should be. As the saying goes, *you do you.*

Pornography reinforces this view of sex. For the past few decades many educators and counselors have promoted porn as a form of positive sex education for children and adults.[3] In my doctoral training in psychology, I was taught to encourage couples to use porn as a way to heighten sexual excitement. The problem is that porn teaches a view of sex that is unrealistic and separated from genuine connection with an actual human being. Porn fuels the belief that great sex is all about your personal experience of easy arousal and orgasm.

When men or women have grown up looking at pornography, they learn to view sex as a consumer. I should get what I want, when I want it, and how I want it. Sex is about obtaining pleasure, excitement, and a release for personal benefit. Porn doesn't ask anything from you but exists to immediately cater to your every sexual fantasy. Porn trains a person's sexual response to be impatient, selfish, and always demanding something more exciting than what you experienced last time.

Clint explains how this played out in his marriage:

When Charity and I got married at twenty-three years old, I was suffering from an addiction to pornography but wouldn't have called it that at the time. I didn't want to let it affect our marriage and resolved that after we said our vows, porn would no longer be a part of my life, and it would stop controlling my thoughts. I prayed that everything I had done would just magically go away and never interfere with my marriage or sexual intimacy with Charity.

Unfortunately, it didn't take long for us to experience porn's effects on our relationship. The very first night, only hours after we said our vows, I was dissatisfied with our sexual experience. I couldn't shake the pornographic thoughts during intercourse and compared Charity's body, her experience, and my experience to what I had watched online for over a decade.

Sadly, I expected that our sex life would look like a pornographic film. I thought sex would be effortless, pain-free, and filled with all kinds of positions and multiple orgasms for both of us. Instead, my wife experienced pain. I made comments about her body that were unkind and constantly compared our experience to what I was exposed to in pornography, leaving me disappointed sexually from our very first night.

Charity recalls me being very disappointed with the frequency of sex, the positions we tried, and me being unable to orgasm or make her climax on cue. We didn't talk about it, and I began to believe that it would always be this way. We both became defeated quickly, and I believed I would never experience anything close to what I thought we were going to have. Eventually, I turned back to pornography and masturbation as a way to cope with feelings of inadequacy and that I was internally flawed.

While you may not have a sexual addiction or history of pornography use like Clint, don't underestimate how society's story of sexual wholeness has impacted your marriage. Many Christian couples believe that their sex life is fundamentally broken if it's not always pleasurable and compatible. Underlying their frustration, they believe: *A great sex life means being married to someone who has a similar sexual appetite. We climax together and have to put forth very little effort to enjoy sex.* I've met with both men and women who contemplate divorce or justify an affair because their sexual needs are not being met within marriage. Often when I speak at events, people share their stories with me. One woman told me bluntly why she felt she was free to have sex with other men. "I haven't been in love with my husband for more than a decade. So in God's eyes, I'm not really married to him anymore."

Having sex with a real person who has feelings and their own sexual needs means you have to be patient, understanding, and unselfish. To the extent that you buy into the culture's story of sex, you will hit a brick wall when you can't make sex "work" in your marriage. At a recent conference, a man told me, "My wife really doesn't turn me on. Sex has never been great. Now we pretty much just avoid it. Honestly, I've learned to meet my own needs through fantasy and masturbation. It's just easier than trying to connect with her. Sometimes I wonder if God has someone else out there for me who would better meet my sexual needs." If sex is less than pleasurable in marriage, what's the point?

> **The culture's greatest fault is not in that it over promises on sex but that it under promises.**

Jordan explains how porn impacted his view of sex: "I dissociated sex from love. It just became a primal instinct. I got to the point where I didn't want to have sex with my wife because sex had become so tarnished that I didn't want to tarnish her."

Another fallout of the culture's view of sex is the emphasis on performance. Both men and women express the pressure to live up to the unrealistic experiences presented by pornography. Cory explained, "I'm always wondering, *Am I good enough?*" His wife Keyla added, "The world presents sex as the secret sauce that you need in life. But it made me view men as cheaters and women as objects."

While the culture's story puts a lot of emphasis on having great sex, it actually misses the beauty of a far deeper intimacy that sex in marriage calls us to pursue. The culture's greatest fault is not in that it over promises on sex but that it under promises. It teaches us to think like three-year-olds who become so fascinated by the wrapping paper that we never think to open the true gift.

THE CHURCH'S STORY OF SEX

I recently posed this question on Facebook: "What did you learn from the church about sex?" Responses came flooding in. About half of them simply said, "Nothing." Here is a sampling of the other responses:

Don't have sex! It's the unforgivable sin.

True love waits. Purity rings. The rose petal being ripped off.

Christians don't talk about sex.

You're broken or used if you have premarital sex.

It happens in marriage, but rarely.

Sex before marriage was forbidden. Girls who got pregnant beforehand were viewed as tramps.

Our pastor said boys need to keep their pants zipped and girls need to keep their legs crossed. The message we seemed to be getting from our youth minister was as long as you don't go all the way, then you're still a virgin.

Don't do it until you're married. Then wives should meet their husband's needs so that they don't "wander" into sin.

It's a sin if you have sex outside of marriage.

If a girl got pregnant, she had to stand in front of the congregation and apologize. Even when our pastor's daughter got pregnant.

From church, I don't recall hearing any teaching about this. From my mom, your virginity is the most valuable thing you have, don't lose it.

Wait until you're married, but after you're married it's fun.

These comments are representative of what I hear everywhere. This is how most of us have learned to think about God and sex.

Let's first address the silence. When you never hear a Christian leader talk candidly about sex, you probably assume that God Himself doesn't have much to say on the topic. Because of the silence from the church on sex, a lot of people don't even consider that God cares about this area of our lives, other than judging us for sexual sin. This means that you are far more likely to look for advice on sex through an internet search than you are from Christian sources.

Second, notice the focus on sexual morality. Sex is viewed first and foremost as a category of good and bad behavior without any explanation of why God tells us to "save sex for marriage." Sexual moral failures are considered the worst kind of sin, described as "unforgivable." This is why we often hide sexual sin instead of seeking help and restoration.

Then there is the disparity between what girls and women learn in the church versus what is taught to boys and men. Women, young and old, are considered the moral gatekeepers of sex. Only guys are supposed to really want sex and are expected to push for it. Once you get married, much of the teaching is around a woman's "marital duty" to her husband. Women are blamed for a husband's porn use and sometimes even for her own sexual trauma because of what she was wearing or for putting herself in a bad situation.

Finally, notice the absence of any clear teaching on what to expect in marriage, other than "it will be fun." There is no mention of the common and real-life struggles of mismatched desires, how to deal with shame or betrayal, and the reality that married sex takes work, commitment, and sacrifice.

The church's traditional story of sex has largely been reduced to biblical warnings about sexual sin and immorality without any explanation of why a loving God would be so mad about our sex lives. "Sexual immorality is bad" has for many been translated as "sexuality is bad." As one secular comedian said, "To hear many religious people talk, one would think God created the torso, head, legs and arms, but the devil slapped on the genitals."[4] We are currently witnessing the fallout of a generation of Christians who grew up hearing only the rules about biblical sexuality without a larger vision for God's purpose and redemption. We will dive into that a bit more in chapter 3.

Before you get too angry with your pastor or parents, realize that they were just repeating the messages that have been passed down from earlier generations. Many Christian leaders throughout modern church history have promoted an incomplete and unbiblical understanding of this beautiful gift from God. Just consider some of these quotes:

"Nothing is so much to be shunned as sexual relations."
—St. Augustine[5]

"Intercourse is never without sin; but God excuses it by his grace because the estate of marriage is his work."
—Martin Luther[6]

"The Holy Spirit leaves the room when a married couple has sex, even if they do it without passion."
—Twelfth-century theologian Peter Lombard[7]

"The wedding day is, ironically, both the happiest and most terrifying day of (a young woman's) life. On the positive side, there is the wedding itself. . . . On the negative side, there is the wedding night, during which the bride must pay the piper, so to speak, by facing for the first time the terrible experience of sex. At this point . . . let me concede one shocking truth. Some young women actually anticipate the wedding night ordeal with curiosity and pleasure! Beware such an attitude! . . . One cardinal rule of marriage should never be forgotten: Give little, give seldom, and above all, give grudgingly."
—A pamphlet for young brides written by a pastor's wife in the late 1800s[8]

Over the years, I've met countless women and men who describe the impact this thinking has had on their sex lives. They all say something similar: "All I ever heard was 'save sex for marriage,' and somehow I was supposed to flip a switch on my wedding day. Well, I've never been able to flip that switch."

As you will read in the next chapter, the Bible says a lot about sex, and it's actually good news for your marriage! I am thrilled to see Christian leaders begin to address sexual issues with candor and the richer message of the Bible. But I don't want to skip over the fact that most of us have to deconstruct some LEGO-like building pieces related to how we view God and sex.

I love God's Word. By calling you to "deconstruct," I by no means am suggesting that you move away from a biblical understanding of sexuality. I'm actually encouraging you to press more deeply into it.

If the sum total of your religious teaching on sex has convinced you that sex itself is shameful, please keep reading! If you believe that God can never truly bless your sex life because of past sin, the Bible has great news for you. If you think that God doesn't care deeply about your sexual pain, I challenge you to rethink your understanding of God. If you believe that God has rejected you because of your particular form of sexual struggle, let's revisit what it means that "Christ Jesus came into the world to save sinners—of whom I am the worst."[9] If you view sexual pleasure as something that your spouse owes you, you're missing the whole purpose of sex in your marriage. And if you think that you and your spouse have experienced God's best just because you don't cheat on each other or fight about sex, get ready for a wonderful surprise!

My friend, God is not a barrier to a fulfilling sex life in your marriage, even if you have received hurtful and incomplete messages from the church. In fact, understanding God's heart for sex is the key to unlocking the power and beauty of this great gift in ways that you may not even be able to imagine.

You and your spouse were created for more than the superficial pleasure of an orgasm. The fullness of God's plan for your marriage is not simply about moral duty and obligation. Sex for you right now may represent anger, disappointment, hurt, shame, and even despair. You may feel hopeless and resigned because you've tried many suggestions of how to have a great sex life.

This is where Ken and Linda were for more than three decades of their marriage. At one point, they had a book burning in their backyard with all of the books they had read on sex and marriage that got them nowhere. They had given up.

What finally made the difference for Linda and Ken was realizing that they were working with the wrong understanding of sexual wholeness, both from a cultural and religious perspective. It's as if their GPS had been hijacked, giving advice that led them to a never-ending series of dead ends.

"Your word is a lamp for my feet, a light on my path."[10] Have you ever considered that this may include God's word to you considering sex in your marriage?

Hidden in the pages of the Bible is a mysterious story of sex that is timeless and full of hope. It will give you an entirely new way of viewing not just the ecstasy of sexual pleasure in your marriage, but also how God can show His goodness through your greatest sexual challenges.

I truly cannot wait to tell you this story!

Chapter 2

God's Story of Sex

Why? Three simple letters that represent the most pressing questions of human existence.

Children begin asking the question *why* almost as soon as they can speak: *Why do I have to go to bed? Why can't I have a cookie?* As they grow and mature, so do their whys. *Why can't I go out with my friends? Why should I care about someone I can't even relate to? Why should I believe in God?*

We never stop asking why. Let's be honest. There seem to be a lot of unanswered whys with sex. *Why would God make sex so difficult to enjoy? Why can't I stop thinking about sex? Why do I feel so much shame about something that happened to me years ago?*

Existential philosopher and Holocaust survivor Viktor Frankl famously quoted Nietzsche: "If you have a why for your life, you can get by with almost any how."[1]

You cannot accurately understand or perhaps even endure the *what* and *how* of sex in your marriage unless you can embrace a compelling *why*. Why does God care about your sex life? And why did He create you as a sexual being?

UNPACKING THE STORY

One day, my teenage son asked me, "Mom, where does the Bible say we shouldn't have sex before marriage?" I could have explained to my son the Greek meaning of the words "fornication" and "sexual immorality" in the many Bible passages that tell us what *not* to do with our sexuality.[2] Instead, I wanted him to begin to understand the story of sex in the Bible. I wanted to share with him the all-important why, not just the cliche, "Because God said so."

God's story of sex is wrapped up in God's larger story told throughout the whole Bible. The Christian Bible is made up of sixty-six books that all tell one amazing story. It begins in the garden of Eden where God created Adam and then Eve. Only two chapters into the Bible, we read that, through Adam and Eve, God introduced marriage and sex: "That is why a man shall leave his father and mother and is united to his wife, and they become one flesh. Adam and his wife were both naked, and they felt no shame" (Gen. 2:24–25). If you only read Genesis, you would think that the main purpose of male and female, sex and marriage, is to have babies and fill the earth. But you have to keep reading.

If you fast-forward all the way to the end of the Bible, you will find the book of Revelation where you read about another wedding: "Let us rejoice and be glad and give him glory! For the wedding of the Lamb has come, and his bride has made herself ready" (Rev. 19:7). This marriage is not between a man and a woman, but between Christ and His bride, the church. The wedding in Revelation ushers in an eternal honeymoon, not with physical sex, but with the spiritual oneness of God and His people. Everything in between Genesis and Revelation connects these two weddings.

Pretty heady stuff, right? So what does that have to do with the why of sex? Paul addressed this question when he wrote to the Ephesian church about marriage. He repeated what happened in Genesis,

"For this reason a man shall leave his father and his mother, and be joined to his wife; and they shall become one flesh."[3] But then Paul expounded, actually explaining the "for this reason." Paul is going to give us the ultimate why of sex. Are you ready?

"This is a profound mystery—but I am talking about Christ and the church."[4]

Okay. Let's take a breath for a minute. I'm so glad Paul used the word "mystery" because it helps validate us when we scratch our heads and say, "What do you mean, Paul?"

Paul is saying the whole Bible is the story of a wedding. From the very beginning of Genesis to the very end of Revelation, we see that God created male and female, the covenant promise of marriage, and the sexual union of husband and wife to be not only sacred, but symbolic.[5] Author and teacher Christopher West explains it this way: "The Bible can be summed up in five words: God wants to marry us."[6]

God embedded within His creation a variety of physical things that point to spiritual truths. Physical hunger and thirst teach us about spiritual hunger and thirst.[7] A family who adopts a child gives us a picture of how God adopts us as His children.[8] God created sexuality and marriage as a physical experience that reveals to us the spiritual truth of how He loves us.

God created sexuality and marriage as a physical experience that reveals to us the spiritual truth of how He loves us.

Think for a moment about the way God designed the physiology of sex. The man is aroused by love and initiates union with his wife. When she feels safe and loved, her body opens to allow him to enter into her and they physically become one. Through the intercourse of becoming one, the man deposits seed in the woman that has the capacity to bring forth life. Now let's apply this as one divine metaphor to Jesus and the church. Jesus initiates love. He sees His Bride as beautiful and pure because of His love for us. When we, the bride, understand His love and protection, we receive Him. He abides in us, becoming one with us. Our union with Christ includes the deposit of the Holy Spirit within us, giving us the capacity to bring forth spiritual life.

As you read this, are you fascinated or weirded out? You've probably spent so many years learning to separate sex from God that it is strange to think about one representing the other. If you do not see God's love for His people as the backdrop to your sexuality, you will be continually confused and frustrated, as I was, in trying to make sense of sex in your marriage.

Think of your sex life as if it is a 5,000-piece jigsaw puzzle. You and your spouse are sorting through the various pieces trying to figure out how they all fit together. The problem is, you don't know what the picture is eventually supposed to look like. Putting together a jigsaw puzzle is infinitely more difficult (if not impossible) if you don't have the correct picture on the front of the box as a reference point, helping you to discern where each piece of the puzzle fits. In Ephesians 5, Paul is saying that the front of the puzzle box is Christ's love for His bride. If you are wondering about some aspect of marriage or sex, look at the picture you are meant to be creating.

During those frustrating years of my marriage, I gave up on sexual intimacy because I didn't see the fullness of what we were supposed to be creating as husband and wife. The books I read were solution focused without giving us a vision for why sex mattered in the first place. I knew enough about the Bible to know that marriage somehow pointed to Christ and church, but I had no idea of how that truth could practically give us hope and a vision for our failing sex life. The puzzle box was at best, fuzzy. We experienced "pieces" of the puzzle that didn't fit within our picture of what God wanted us to work toward. Understanding sex as a metaphor for the mystery of Christ's love has given context and purpose to even the difficult seasons of our marriage.

Honestly, I've been unpacking this mystery for the past decade. If this is the first time you've heard this story of sex and God, give yourself some time to let it settle in. The rest of this book will help you wrestle through how God's covenant love gives context to the real-life joys and challenges of your sex life.

WHAT IS COVENANT LOVE?

One of the challenges to grasping God's story of sex is that we often misunderstand the relationship between sex and love. We get sex wrong because we so often get love wrong.

Caleb and Jackie got married because they "fell in love" with each other. Eleven years into marriage, their love is fading. Instead of talking together in the evenings, they typically retreat to their phones. Caleb and Jackie have sex about once every week or two, rarely with passion and only when Caleb initiates. Both of them silently wonder, "Have we just fallen out of love?" Falling in love means you can also fall out of it.

What Caleb and Jackie understand as "love" is not what's on the front of the puzzle box. God didn't create sex *primarily* to teach us about romantic love, passion, or even unselfishness, although each of those are important ingredients we will get to in future chapters. The larger vision that puts all of the ingredients together is **covenant love**.

A covenant is a unique type of relationship. Most relationships we have with people are at some level contractual. Although you don't spell out what you each bring to the table, there is an unspoken understanding that your relationship will only last as long as it is mutually beneficial. Friends come and go through different seasons. Even your closest friends twenty years ago probably aren't in your life today. You simply outgrew the benefits of the friendship and moved on. Most of us think of marriage with this type of contractual mindset.[9]

Take Caleb and Jackie as an example. Caleb was drawn to Jackie because of her stunning beauty and fun personality. These qualities made Caleb *feel* love for Jackie. He loved being with her. He stood a bit taller when his friends commented on Jackie's beauty. "Wow. She's out of your league!"

Jackie fell in love because of Caleb's thoughtfulness. She loved how he took time to think through important issues and went out of his way to make her feel special. Caleb was the first person in the world who really seemed to notice Jackie for more than a pretty face.

As in every marriage, the qualities that initially drew Caleb and Jackie together faded with familiarity. Jackie settled into motherhood and now doesn't have the energy to style her hair, put on makeup, and dress in the latest fashions like she once did. Her fun-loving personality now annoys Caleb more than helping him "lighten up." And Jackie doesn't feel much love for Caleb anymore. He doesn't do the sweet things he once did, like bringing her flowers or rubbing her feet at the end of a long day. He's always lost in his thoughts and hardly notices her. Caleb and Jackie might read a marriage book or go to a counselor to try to resurrect the *feelings* of love they once had. What they don't recognize is that they need to embrace a different kind of love . . . covenant love.

Pastor and author Tim Keller defines a covenant as "the solemn, permanent, whole self-giving of two parties to each other. It is a stunning blend of both law and love . . . a relationship much more intimate and loving than a mere legal contract could create, yet one more enduring and binding than personal affection alone could make."[10]

In a society that values immediate gratification and quickly discards anything that is uncomfortable, covenant love can appear to be very unromantic. One young husband honestly shared this: "The word 'covenant' doesn't sound very lovely. It sounds like a chore or a follow-through on something you don't really want anymore." Yet, covenant is the love we all long for. It is why marriage holds a different hope and promise than any other relationship.

In marriage, we generally choose to love one another as long as we are meeting each other's needs. Covenant love flips this on its head. We meet each other's needs because we have chosen to love. A covenant is a different kind of love because it is based on a promise. God loves with covenant love. He is the Father who gives good gifts to His children. He is the parent who loves enough to discipline His sons and daughters. But He is also the husband who pursues His bride, sacrificed His life for her, and loves her with an eternal, faithful, and unfailing love.

In the Old Testament, God's "marriage" covenant was with the Israelites, His chosen people. Isaiah wrote, "Your Maker is your husband—the LORD Almighty is His name—the Holy One of Israel is your Redeemer" (Isa. 54:5). If you've read the Old Testament, you know that the Israelites didn't want a covenant marriage with God. They wanted a contract, only worshiping Him when He was giving them what they demanded. They wanted the good gifts of God, but not God Himself. The Israelites loved God with a very fickle love and ended up breaking their covenant repeatedly by giving their love to other gods.

When Jesus died and was resurrected, He did so to usher in a new and more complete covenant.[11] Now, God's covenant love is with those who trust in Jesus Christ. Think about this for a minute. Just as a husband "leaves his father and mother to be one with his wife," Jesus left His heavenly Father to become one with His church. I know it's difficult to grasp, but everything about marriage and sex is God's revelation to us about His covenant love.

God wants us within marriage to move past contractual, fickle love into embracing a true covenant. You don't know if you have covenant love in your marriage until every other facet of love like romantic feelings and attraction begin to fade away. Only then are you left with the choice to love as Jesus loves.

God created marriage and sex this way to reveal Himself through the day-to-day relationship of a husband and wife walking out their covenant. Even if you are not a Christian, your emotions, longings, and sexuality speak of this. A "good marriage" is written on our hearts and minds to include tenderness, mutual sexual pleasure, unselfishness, and above all, faithfulness. Even amid a sexual revolution, over ninety percent of Americans still believe it is morally wrong to cheat on your spouse.[12] Why? Because covenant love is embedded in our hearts. We long for an eternal, faithful, passionate love. We write novels about it, sing songs about it, and feel desperately unsatisfied when we fail to experience it. The end result of these longings was never meant to be a great marriage. The best experiences in marriage were created to point us toward the eternal covenant love of God.

> The best experiences in marriage were created to point us toward the eternal covenant love of God.

For the sake of what they think is love, many married couples sabotage their covenant. When the romantic feelings wane and attraction fades, sex becomes absent or shallow. Both husband and wife can be emotionally or sexually drawn to other lovers. What they fail to understand is that true sexual intimacy is less an expression of the love we feel than the investment in the love we have chosen.

When my son asked me where the Bible says to save sex for marriage, he was looking for the rule without a vision for the beauty. The Bible calls us to save sex for marriage, not primarily because of the sacredness of sex, but because of the beauty of covenant. God created sex to be the most tangible expression of the joy of fully giving oneself in covenant. In contrast, sex apart from marriage fuels our self-obsession and the belief that "finding love" is all about temporarily feeling good. Sex and marriage go together because sex is the physical symbol of the lifelong covenant promise. It is how we celebrate and remember with our bodies what we have chosen to do with our entire lives.[13] (We will dive into this more in chapter 7.) If our understanding of love is wrong, the outworking of sex in marriage will also be skewed.

> **The Bible calls us to save sex for marriage, not primarily because of the sacredness of sex, but because of the beauty of covenant.**

Unfortunately, even within marriage, most of us still work with an immature understanding of love and sex. We can't move past the disappointment of the kind of love we imagined marriage and sex were supposed to offer. Ironically, it is only the temporary absence of romantic and erotic love that ushers in the possibility of developing the kind of love Christ has for us! Hitting a wall in your sex life may feel like the end of natural love, but it might just be the invitation to discover covenant.

Jackie and Caleb have a choice to make. They can continue to ride the wave of fleeting feelings for each other or fight their way through disappointment toward covenant love. It is only when Caleb isn't automatically attracted to Jackie that he can pursue her with the passion that comes from covenant. It is only when Jackie feels neglected by her husband's absent-mindedness that the love of Christ can compel her to be vulnerable and patient.

SEX IS UNDER ATTACK

I look forward to making this very practical for your marriage in the chapters that follow. But before moving on, I want you to understand an important aspect of God's story of sex: it is constantly under spiritual attack.

As you read about God's beautiful story of sex, you might be thinking: *What you are describing is so far from my experience! Sex throughout my life has been a lot more like a nightmare. I can't even begin to wrap my mind around the idea that sex has something to do with God's love.*

There is a reason that most of us have great trouble accepting God's story of sex. While you might just be learning about the spiritual significance of sex, Satan has known this all along. He understands that when we experience sex as it was intended, we will have a tangible and powerful picture of God's great covenant love. Satan will do anything he can to separate you from experiencing the fullness of sexual intimacy in your marriage.

Christopher West explains this attack on our intimacy:

If the body and sex are meant to proclaim our union with God, and if there's an enemy who wants to separate us from God, what do you think he's going to attack? If we want to know what's most sacred in this world, all we need do is look for what is most violently profaned. The enemy is no dummy. He knows that the body and sex are meant to proclaim the divine mystery. And from his perspective, this proclamation must be stifled. Men and women must be kept from recognizing the mystery of God in their bodies.[14]

The beautiful story of sexuality has been repeatedly distorted to the point where many of us can't identify what it was originally created to represent. I think of a mature Christian woman who, because of horrific childhood abuse, believes sex will always be dirty and tainted with pain and violence. Or a young husband who was so scarred by porn use that he can't be sexual without thinking about a twisted sexual scenario.

The spiritual battle for God's story of sex is not just "out there" with the obvious evils of human trafficking or child abuse. Satan is also working by telling lies, distracting you with the world's version of sex, or discouraging you through legalistic teaching that makes you believe you can never be forgiven. Satan has a huge win when a Christian husband and wife resent each other because of sex. He gets the victory in our secret choices to flirt with sexual sin and in the self-righteous bitterness of a spouse who can't forgive.

The spiritual battle around sexuality is an important why behind your pain and frustration. It is also the why that will compel you to fight for your sex life.

The story of sex in your marriage is intended to reflect the greatest story of all time. Every marriage faces unique challenges to do this. At every stage of struggle, you are invited to connect your broken story of sex to the story of God's covenant love. The classic fairytale couple who falls in love, has no problems, and experiences great sex all the time may be an alluring storyline to pursue. The story of God is messier and far richer than that. It's about a love that transcends all brokenness, selfishness, and sin.

You might be able to boil the messiness of your sex life down to a misunderstanding of covenant love, like Jackie and Caleb experienced. But for many couples, the brokenness of their sex life is further complicated by wounds, past choices, and shame that make God's story of sex seem unattainable.

I could give you hundreds of examples of couples who are buried beneath the real-life struggles of sex in marriage. Each story is different, but they all represent frustration, shame, and pain. Reading that "sex is a beautiful picture of God's covenant love" may feel like salt in a wound. But as couples just like you and your spouse surrender their broken story of sex to God's picture of covenant love, they can begin to walk into deeper levels of intimacy than they ever imagined possible.

Just knowing what your sex life is designed to look like can provide the hope of a framework to be working toward. Jannette shared how she is experiencing this hope:

I started reading the book, *God, Sex, and Your Marriage* with a poisoned perspective about sex and sexuality. So poisoned that I just couldn't believe God wanted anything to do with my mess. The truth is that God wants everything to do with my mess because He wants me to know the truth about His perspective on sex. There is healing in knowing His perspective. There is hope in knowing His perspective.

Her husband, Francisco, echoed that new understanding of sex within covenant love:

I am a recovering sex addict. I had been a sex addict for thirty-seven years. As I grew up I longed for real love but never had the right image of it. All I knew was the distorted messages from pornography and culture; objectification of women, emotional detachment, and selfish self-satisfaction. When I got married, I brought all of that imagery and fantasy with me. It almost destroyed our marriage. I am learning that sex is a living metaphor of God's deep love for us. I am finally gaining the right imagery of sex in my mind to replace all the space taken up by porn. I understand how selflessness, self-control, and vulnerability are key elements to a healthy sex life. Marriage is a covenant of love; sex is a joyful celebration of that covenant.

As Jannette and Francisco are learning, God's power to redeem is greater than Satan's power to destroy. God created sex to be a beautiful picture of His love. Our sin and Satan's schemes have ruined that picture. Yet, Jesus came to redeem every aspect of our humanity, including sexuality. Your marriage is meant to tell *that story*, first to one another, and then to a world desperate for hope.

Are you ready to start writing it?

Chapter 3

Wholeness Beyond Sexual Purity

We made it! Just barely, but we managed to follow the rule of saving sex for our wedding night. It felt a bit like crawling across the finish line to get God's "good job" as we said, "I do."

We left our wedding late into the evening and went to a swanky local hotel with visions of marriage bliss. As with many newlyweds, things didn't go as planned. Our evening began with an elderly bellman who took an extraordinary amount of time to show us around the hotel room, including how to watch different TV channels (I'm not kidding!). Then, about thirty minutes later, at a very inopportune time, the bellman knocked on our door to tell us that he'd found the champagne that was part of our honeymoon package. With hindsight, I suspect that this was all part of his plan to sabotage honeymoons.

I wish I could tell you that things got better, but they didn't. We drove to my in-laws' cabin in Tennessee for the rest of our honeymoon where there literally was no bed. Mike and I slept (and tried other things) on an air mattress on top of hardwood floors. Now, twenty-seven years later, I can tell you that we were unable to have intercourse through most of our honeymoon. (I was so humiliated by this that I couldn't even tell my closest friends.) When we did finally have sex, it hurt. And the hurt didn't go away. For decades, I experienced pain during intercourse.

Growing up, I had been told that sex was an amazing gift from God for married couples. Why would God give me a gift that included so much pain and disappointment? I decided that sex is only a gift for some people (mostly men), but certainly not for me. Sex instead became a sign of my love for my husband. Would I be willing to endure pain for the sake of his pleasure? I stayed stuck in this thinking for many, many years.

How I wish I could talk to that young couple on their honeymoon. Or that struggling husband and wife parenting young children who felt so stuck in this area of marriage. I would start by telling them this: honoring God with your sexuality is not just about keeping rules or performing a duty, but about a wholehearted pursuit of God's character through this journey.

LET'S TALK ABOUT PURITY

You may have noticed that there is a lot of criticism directed toward teaching on sexual purity. Within the past several years, hundreds of blogs and dozens of books have been written documenting the harmful effects of what is now called "purity culture." Beginning in the 1990s, Christian resources teaching teens and young adults about sex centered around this concept of sexual purity. "Save sex for your wedding night. It will be worth it!"

The Bible without exception tells us to run from every form of sexual immorality.[1] Christians are also called to pursue purity and holiness as a response to God's love for us.[2] Sexual sin can have devastating effects on our body, future relationships, and emotional well-being. However, we have to be careful to understand sexual struggles and sin within the more important message of Christ's salvation, healing, and redemption.

While the encouragement to save sex for marriage is a biblical one, some elements of purity-focused teaching built an entire theology on one aspect of God and sex: good Christians don't have sex outside of marriage. The good news of the gospel and God's heart for our redemption got lost in a one-dimensional message that subtly equated virginity with salvation. Purity messages also fail to give Christian married couples a vision for what it means to fully honor God with their sexuality. Sexual wholeness involves far more than just avoiding sin. What Mike and I ran into in our marriage is just one example of how reducing biblical sexuality to "saving sex for marriage" has confused and misguided both married and single Christians. This simplistic approach to God and sex has unfortunately caused ongoing shame and unresolved pain for many, many people.

> **Purity messages also fail to give Christian married couples a vision for what it means to fully honor God with their sexuality. Sexual wholeness involves far more than just avoiding sin.**

There is much more to God's gift of sex than the formula "sexual purity will result in a great marriage." Before we dive into what God designed your sex life to look like, here are a few important clarifications if you have been impacted negatively by purity culture.

Your salvation and purity are not based on your sexual choices.

Let me ask you a question. Are you sexually pure? There is a good chance you don't even know how to answer that question. Does your purity have to do with whether or not you had sex before you got married? Or whether or not you've ever sought out pornography or cheated on your spouse?

I have bad news and good news for you. The bad news is that you've blown it. God's standard of purity, sexual and otherwise, is so high that you cannot possibly keep it. Jesus made this point: "You have heard that it was said, 'You shall not commit adultery.' But I tell you that anyone who looks at a woman lustfully has already committed adultery with her in his heart" (Matt. 5:27–28). With this statement, Jesus moved the achievable standard of sexually pure behavior to the impossible standard of absolute purity in our sexual thoughts.

I shared with you at the beginning of this chapter that Mike and I did not have sex together before we got married. Yes, I was technically a virgin. But as my understanding of God's design for sexuality has expanded, so has my awareness of how terribly I've missed that mark, both before and within marriage.

The Bible clearly reminds us that none of us can ever become "pure" because of our choices to avoid sin. "There is no one righteous, not even one. . . . All have turned away, they have together become useless" (Rom. 3:10–12). The "purest" people in Jesus' day were the religious leaders. You've probably heard them called "Pharisees." They would have been the ones harshly judging people who admitted to masturbating or sleeping around. The Pharisees followed the rules of the Bible with meticulous care. They were also the people to whom Jesus had the most critical things to say. They looked good on the outside, but they didn't realize the rottenness of their own hearts. It's ultimately not an affair, premarital sex, or pornography that makes us impure. Those actions are the symptoms of a disordered heart that has rejected God.

That's the bad news. Give up on purity because it's impossible.

But there is actually some great news. I am totally and completely pure (sexually and otherwise), and you can be too! My purity hasn't been accomplished by following the rules, but through the fact that

I have trusted in the Lord Jesus Christ as my sole source of purity. It is only by faith in Jesus that any of us can be pure, and when we trust in Him, we take on His purity in exchange for all of our sin.[3]

You may have heard this message before, but do you really believe it? Let's compare two people. One has never looked at porn, saved sex for marriage, and thinks only sexually about his or her spouse. The other began having sex at the age of thirteen and has had more sexual partners, male and female, than you could count. Sex for this person has been a stumbling journey toward understanding God's design in marriage. Both of these people place their trust in Jesus Christ, repenting of their sins and giving their heart to God. *Is one more sexually pure than the other?* The answer is no!

In 1 Corinthians 6:11, Paul tells us that we all came out of various sinful lifestyles. That is who we *were*, but no longer who we *are* in Christ Jesus: "But you were washed, you were sanctified, you were justified in the name of the Lord Jesus Christ and by the Spirit of our God."

Do you feel self-righteous because you saved sex for marriage and your spouse didn't? Or do you feel like you are forever tainted, undeserving of love because of your past sexual sin?

Being a Christian truly means that we become new people in the eyes of God. In fact, we are told to not look at people (including ourselves or our spouse) in the light of how the world sees things. Instead, we realize that our worth, our purity, and our salvation comes through our relationship with God. Everything about our old lives is gone! Forgiveness and freedom are real!

So many men and women see themselves as "second-class Christians" because of their sexual past. This is not an accurate way of viewing ourselves or others. Friend, stop trying to earn God's favor by cleaning up your thoughts and behaviors.

In 1 Corinthians 6, Paul teaches that our new identity in Christ results in a life surrendered to God, including how we steward our sexuality. "You are not your own; you were bought at a price. There-fore honor God with your bodies."[4] In the chapters that follow, we will look at what it means to honor God as you navigate sex in your marriage. Without question, God calls His people to walk in holi-ness, sexually and otherwise. But we steward our sex lives because of God's love, never to earn it.

The "reward" for following God is not necessarily a great sex life.

Some have described purity culture as prosperity gospel applied to sex. In other words, God wants you to be happy. If you do things His way, He will give you everything your heart desires. The impli-cation is that honoring God with your sex life will result in sexual utopia in marriage.

I have heard from hundreds of couples who are grappling with how this "formula" of "honoring God = great sex" has broken down for them. A woman married a pastor only to be repeatedly betrayed by him. A man saved sex for marriage and now lives with a wife who hates sex. Couples who wonder if their infertility is somehow linked to the fact that they had sex together before marriage.

God created the natural world with built-in consequences for our choices. The book of Proverbs is essentially the encouragement to live within the wisdom of God's created order. If you eat junk food, you probably won't be healthy. If you gossip, you won't have close friends. If you nag your husband, he's not likely to spend a lot of time at home. If you ignore your wife's emotional needs, don't expect her to be eager to meet yours. That's all great advice and sound wisdom.

Solomon applies the sow-reap principles of wisdom to our sexual choices as well. In Proverbs 5, 6, and 7, he warns about the relational and spiritual consequences of sexual sin. "Can a man scoop fire into his lap without his clothes being burned? Can a man walk on hot coals without his feet being scorched? So is he who sleeps with another man's wife; no one who touches her will go unpunished" (Prov. 6:27–29).

Yes, there are consequences for all of our choices, including sexual choices. Sexually Transmitted Diseases (STDs) are a real thing. Having multiple sexual partners means bringing memories of intimacy with other people into your marriage. Looking at pornography wires your sexual drive to unrealistic images and will undermine your sexual response to your spouse. What we sow, we reap. Unfortunately, we may also experience the fallout of others' unwise and sinful choices. God's design that we save sex for marriage can spare us and those we love from the pain of these consequences. It is wise to have only one sexual partner—your spouse.

But natural consequences and spiritual blessing are two different things. There are natural benefits that can (but not always will) come from following God's design. While this is a principle of wisdom, God doesn't promise this specific reward. There are many examples of people who followed the rules (sow) and experienced sexual pain and brokenness (reap). There are other examples of people who didn't follow the rules, but seem to be thriving. God does promise that He is a refuge for those who trust in Him.[5] When you surrender your life to God, including your sexuality, you can have confidence that God is with you no matter what trials you might face. You are walking in His will, even if that means difficult circumstances. God promises to remove the most important consequence of our sin: shame. "Therefore, there is now *no condemnation* for those who are in Christ Jesus" (Rom. 8:1, emphasis added).

This is why David could rejoice at God's forgiveness for his sexual sin, even though he still dealt with some very real consequences. "Blessed is the one whose transgressions are forgiven, whose sins are covered. Blessed is the one whose sin the LORD does not count against them and in whose spirit is no deceit" (Ps. 32:1–2). David knew that God was with him, strengthening him, even as he waded through the painful consequences of his past.

The purity culture (and all forms of prosperity gospel) confuses the promises of God, elevating the *presents* of God above the *presence* of God. Surrendering your sex life to God (before or throughout marriage) doesn't mean a pain-free, euphoric sex life. It does mean that you never have to doubt God's presence with you and goodness toward you in the midst of your circumstances.

God not only calls you to sexual morality, but also wants to grow you in sexual maturity.

Jackson and Daphne have been married for sixteen years. They would describe their sex life as "pretty normal." They have sex once or twice a week, based on how crazy work and family life have been. Sex isn't great, but it "gets the job done." There's very little variety or communication other than "Want to do it tonight?" and "Thanks. That was fun."

If this couple met with their pastor for pastoral counseling, they would probably get a clean bill of sexual health. Neither of them is cheating on the other, and they have semi-regular consensual sex.

> **Understanding God's story of sex presents a vision for what God wants us to move *toward*, not just the sin or brokenness He wants us to move *away from*.**

While Jackson and Daphne are following the rules and expectations of Christian sex, they aren't exactly maturing in their sexual intimacy. Sexual maturity is not simply the absence of problems. It means progressively moving toward the beautiful gift sexual intimacy was created to be. Understanding God's story of sex presents a wonderful and challenging vision for what God wants us to move *toward*, not just the sin or brokenness He wants us to move *away from*.

Purity culture views the wedding day as the end of the journey. "The work is over. No more self-denial. You get the prize at the end of the race!" God's story of sex views the wedding day as a continuation of what it looks like to honor God with your sexuality. Married sex still calls for our effort, intention, and even self-denial with the goal of unfolding the beautiful metaphor of sexual intimacy and covenant love.

Striving for sexual maturity means that every year, through every season, you will have a deeper understanding and experience of sexual intimacy. Even when your bodies age and begin to fail, you will know a depth of love through your sexual journey that you couldn't begin to understand as a young married couple.

I think back to where Mike and I were as a young couple struggling with our issues in marriage. All we knew was to avoid sin and make sex a priority. No one gave us a blueprint for how to address sex beyond that. I had no idea that by settling for a passionless, frustrating sex life we were missing God's work in this area of our lives and marriage. This is why I find it much more helpful to talk about *sexual integrity* than simply *sexual purity*.

WHAT IS SEXUAL INTEGRITY?

We get the word "integrity" from the Latin word *integer*. Integer means to be "whole or undivided." The opposite of integrity is when something or someone is inconsistent, having parts that are splintered off from the whole.

Jesus reminded His disciples that the greatest commandment is the one that the Lord set up continually for the Israelites: "Love the LORD your God with all your heart, with all your soul, and with all your strength."[6] Notice that word "all." To be a Christian means to be a man or woman of integrity. We strive to love God with all of who we are. There is no room for the ten percent that is too personal or costly to surrender to God. I love how missionary Hudson Taylor put it: "Christ is either Lord of all or He is not Lord at all!"[7]

For you to live with sexual integrity means that your sex life is an accurate reflection of the most important thing about you: you are a child of God, made in His image, created to bring glory to Him. God fundamentally changes what we do only by foundationally changing who we are. Christianity is not a call to manage your sin, but an invitation to a new identity through Jesus Christ.

So, what does that practically look like "between the sheets"? Applying this to your marriage, God calls you to steward sex in a manner that represents His divine story.

Integrity means inviting God into your sex life.

When I speak to groups of married Christians, I often ask "How many of you have ever prayed together about your sex life?" Usually, about ten percent of couples raise their hands. Keep in mind, these are Christians who have chosen to attend a conference or workshop about God and sex. Yet, around ninety percent admit that they have never prayed together about sex. They have never asked God to bless them as they share their bodies with one another. They have never thanked God for the gift of pleasure and oneness they just experienced. They have never asked God for help to keep their thoughts honoring to each other and to Him.

You learned in the last chapter that holy sexuality is under constant satanic attack. Yet, we never think to invite God to fight for us, to strengthen us, to heal us, and to help us in this most personal and sacred space. Why?

Most of us would admit that sexuality feels like an area of our lives and marriages that is more "split off" from rather than integrated into our walk with God. This is partially because of the silence about sex most of us have experienced within the church. We may think that if God's messengers (like pastors and teachers) don't talk about sex, then God must not care about it very much. Does He really want us to pray about it?

I think there are even deeper reasons why we don't invite God into our sex lives . . . either within the church conversation or in the privacy of our own bedrooms. Sex is often associated with shame. In Genesis, we read that Adam and Eve were naked and felt no shame.[8] Since sin entered the world, nakedness has been linked with shame. Because of sin, our natural instinct is to hide from each other and to hide from God, especially when we feel the most vulnerable.

Integrity begins by tearing down the barriers that keep God and sex as separate categories in your thinking. Sexuality was not intended to be a secret or shameful compartment of your life. It was created to be the outflow of God's image in you, His love for you, and your love for Him. When Jesus sets us free, when He cleanses us, this extends to every area of our lives.

In Psalm 139, David marvels at the thought that God is always with him. "Where can I go from your Spirit? Where can I flee from your presence?" Do you think God leaves when you and your spouse have sex? Does God's Spirit fly out of the room because He can't stand to see you naked? David also comments on the fact that God knows his thoughts before he even thinks them. Is God unaware of your sexual temptations, your bitterness, or those sexual images that keep flooding your mind?

One young husband shared with me how he had compartmentalized his sexual sin and shame. A week before his wedding, he paid for a lap dance at a strip club. Filled with shame, he shoved the memory away hoping that it wouldn't impact his marriage. He reminded himself that God forgives and redeems, so he should just be able to "move on." But the act haunted him:

The shame and conviction became heavier every day, especially when my wife wanted to be sexually intimate! Here was my beautiful bride, desiring to be one sexually, and there I am with this lie, denying its power over me yet completely controlled by it and afraid to open my mouth for fear of its consequences.

No wonder I couldn't walk in integrity! That would have required me to be whole, and I had never lived like that. Sexual acts: masturbation, pornography, and other unwanted behaviors were always compartmentalized. I had hoped that I could live a married life the way I had led my single life. Compartmentalized and divided. The opposite of an integrated, whole, undivided life.

Friend, God is intimately involved in every area of your life, whether or not you are aware of Him. This should not be an embarrassing or condemning realization. God is your strength, your wisdom, your Counselor, your healer, and your Redeemer. To the extent that you have uninvited Him into your sex life, you are missing His power and redemption. To be a Christian with sexual integrity means no more walls up, no "do not enter" signs, no hiding but giving God the complete permission to redeem, heal, awaken, and transform the good gift of sex in your marriage.

Integrity means your sex life will resemble God's design.

In the last chapter, I used the example of a jigsaw puzzle to describe your sex life. You learned that the picture God wants you to pursue in your sexuality is one that reflects His covenant love. This means that as you and your spouse grapple with the very real issues of sexual pleasure, pain, and frustration in your marriage, your reference point will always be "How does God love His covenant people? How does Jesus love His bride?" In everything, keep referring back to that picture on the front of the puzzle box. When sex feels broken, don't define health as the world does, but pursue the fullness that is expressed in God's love.

"How does God's love help me know what to do with our mismatched sexual desire or the fact that my body isn't cooperating with what my mind wants it to do?" Sex is earthy and complicated. God's love feels ethereal. It's a nice thought but doesn't seem as if it could be practically helpful, right?

Often, we don't see the metaphor of marriage and God's love because we don't know God very well. But the Bible gives us some incredibly tangible handles to understanding God's love.

Pursuing sexual integrity as a married couple means that your sex life will increasingly be characterized by four qualities or pillars that are true about the way God loves His people. In the next section, we will look at each of these qualities as they apply to your sex life. Here is a glimpse of where we are headed:

Pillar 1—Faithfulness

God's covenant love is based on a promise: "I will never leave you or forsake you. I will be your God and you will be my people."[9] God's love for us isn't based on how He is feeling on a given day, but on His character. He will be faithful to what He has promised to do.

The same is true of your marriage covenant with one another. Your covenant is only as strong as your character to walk out what you have promised to each other. Sexual fidelity is the clearest way to keep or to break that covenant promise. Will you be faithful to give yourself only to one another, in good times and bad?

Pillar 2—Intimate Knowing

Our relationship with God is a journey of knowing Him more completely. Every day presents opportunities to step into deeper intimacy with God or to put up walls. The same is true of your sex life. Sexual intimacy isn't just "having sex," but the intentional act of sharing mind, body, and soul. Sexual integrity means choosing to move toward each other, rather than putting up walls. Every day offers you opportunities to walk toward intimate knowing.

Pillar 3—Sacrificial Giving

God's love for humanity throughout history has been one of patient kindness. The climax of His love was the cross where Jesus suffered and died because of love for the Father and for His bride. Why then are we surprised when marriage and sex ask us to sacrifice for one another? Sex is perhaps the most tangible area of your marriage through which you can learn to live out the unselfish love God has for you.

Pillar 4—Passionate Celebration

Your relationship with God was never meant to be one of stoic duty. The word "worship" appears in the Bible over eight thousand times.[10] Just flip through the Psalms and notice the passion with which God's people are meant to express their love! Let's apply that to marriage. Sex is one of the most profound ways we celebrate covenant love. God created the orgasm, the clitoris, and the sensitive nerve endings on the penis for a reason. He designed sex to be pleasurable, passionate, fun, and exciting because it is the celebration of your covenant.

Sexual integrity means that you and your spouse will be working toward each of these four pillars of covenant love. This is what a great sex life is designed to look like. This is what is on "the front of the box"!

Richard shared how viewing sex through this lens has transformed his perspective:

I have completely missed God's design for sex in my life and marriage. My early negative sexual experiences led to me believing lies and feelings of inadequacies. Sex then was why I felt bad about who I was, so I made a vow and separated off sex as something to fix as the way and means for me to feel good about myself. The cultural messages of selfish sex only reinforced my belief in sex as the way to personal fulfillment and happiness.

I became a Christian as a young adult and I believed the purity culture message that if I avoided premarital sex then sex in my marriage would give me this personal fulfillment and satisfaction that I was seeking. Yet my heart was lacking an understanding of God's design and I was using sex and my wife as the way and means for me to fix myself and feel good about myself. Over time, our sex life fell apart and left us feeling depleted and in conflict.

When I first heard of how sexual intercourse can be seen as a metaphor and illustration of how God wants to "marry me" and intimately know me, this completely deconstructed what I believed about sex. Instead of connecting sex to my source of inadequacy, I am connecting sex as a way and means to intimately know and appreciate God and my wife.

As I am constructing this puzzle with the new "true north" related to God's design for sex, I'm feeling less conflict around sex. In addition, I feel more united around "what is our completed puzzle picture on the box?" and "what are we going for?" I see these pillars of covenant love working out in sometimes complex, messy, and hard ways that I don't always understand.

In the chapters that follow, you will learn about these four pillars of covenant love. You will undoubtedly run into aspects of sex that you realized, "That's not where we are." Your sex life may feel very broken right now. As you read about what healthy sexuality was designed to be like, you might begin to feel discouraged. The barriers you and your spouse are facing may seem insurmountable.

That's okay. Remember that you are working on a "puzzle" together. You're on a learning and growing journey.

Kelly describes how she and her husband Scott are navigating the journey together:

Scott and I have been married for nineteen years and all the years have been a struggle sexually. I came in with sexual trauma and he with pornography. I was unable to have sex without a coping mechanism of alcohol and or prescription drugs to numb. When I became fully sober two years ago, intimacy stopped, and we were headed for divorce.

In the beginning of this year, Scott went away to a men's intensive with Be Broken Ministry and at the same time I was doing the Passion Pursuit study. We both were learning the same truths at the same time and when he returned, he was treating me differently than ever before. He spoke honestly and remorsefully about his pornography use and how it has injured me; he apologized and asked for forgiveness. He was making time with me a priority, we were taking walks each night and praying together, he was kissing me goodbye each morning and blessing me.

The care and gentleness that Scott was treating me with made me feel safer than I had ever felt before. One night, he gave me a massage as a gift of love without any expectations for sex. When he was done with the massage, I said, "I think I would like to try to be intimate tonight." He was surprised of course but then I said, "Do you mind if we pray for protection and blessing from God beforehand?," and we prayed together.

From the time I was in third grade and exposed repeatedly to pornography, horrible and shameful pictures had been programmed in and occupied my brain during sex, but not this time, and I was able to experience shame-free intimacy with my husband for the first time. I believe God did protect and bless us, and as we lay there, we both knew that something very different and supernatural had happened.

That month was the absolute best time of our entire marriage. I felt free, safe, and whole, and Scott felt loved and accepted and good enough. I had zero impure images and Scott and I both felt and experienced what a holy marriage and intimacy was like. Sadly, as soon as it came, it also left again and we are back to where we are today, discouraged and hopeless. What changed? I believe that we both have not finished our individual healing work and we stopped being intentional and putting forth the effort it required to experience intimacy outside of the bedroom but expected it to continue inside the bedroom.

I do believe however that God wanted to show us a glimpse and give us a taste of what real, God-given intimacy is supposed to be, and give us the hope to keep fighting for our marriage and our family. Like the Israelite spies who brought back the fruit of the Promised Land as proof, we must decide whether we are going to walk into that land and enjoy the fruit of God's blessing or go back to Egypt despite all that God has shown to us is possible. It requires self-giving love on both of our parts, and when we gave it to each other that month, we experienced true intimacy.

Integrity means that you don't give up on that journey but stay committed to moving toward what God designed sexual intimacy to be. You didn't get where you are in a day. It will take time to build something new; be patient with yourself and with your spouse. Just keep building.

Integrity means recognizing that marriage and sex matter so much because of what they point to.

This last aspect of sexual integrity might surprise you. The covenant of marriage and the beauty of true sexual intimacy are sacred gifts from God. We honor them and value them, understanding that they point to the most important truth in all of history: God created us for Himself. He loves us and pursues us with faithful, sacrificial, and passionate love. We were made to know Him and be known by Him for all of eternity!

There is a danger of valuing marriage and intimacy so highly that we forget it was designed to be a metaphor pointing to something even greater.

As you and your spouse surrender this area of your hearts to the Lord, you *will experience* healing and redemption. But it still won't be perfect. Those moments of deep connection, euphoric excitement, and gleeful laughter will be wonderful, but may be rare and fleeting. Yes, this is because you are two sinful, fallen human beings living in a broken world. But even beyond that, God did not create you for great sex. He didn't even create you for a wonderful marriage. He created you for intimacy with Himself.

I know couples in their seventies and eighties who are in the process of losing one another. For many of them, intercourse isn't possible anymore. They are beyond worrying about the wrinkles and sexual impotency. Now, they worry about the cancer that threatens to take the one they love. They secretly imagine how lonely it will be to one day soon wake up in an empty bed. Even if they enjoyed decades of marriage and sexual pleasure together, it's all fading away now.

"Well, that's a depressing thought, Juli!" Yes, it is, but it's also something that wisdom keeps in mind, "It is better to go to a house of mourning than to go to a house of feasting, for death is the destiny of everyone; the living should take this to heart."[11]

Our ache for the perfect love that is out of reach and our fear of losing the goodness of what we possess remind us of this truth: marriage and sex are temporary gifts meant to awaken our desire for a greater reality.

Jesus said that there will be no marriage in heaven, but we will be like the angels.[12] Why? Because we no longer need the metaphor of God's love when we are alive in His presence. There will be deep intimacy and significant relationships in heaven, but they will not take the form of marriage because marriage is a revelation, pointing us to something in the future. Think of sexual intimacy like a trailer for a movie. It whets your appetite for something . . . giving you just a taste of what will soon be available in its fullness.

C. S. Lewis wrote, "Love ceases to be a demon only when it ceases to be a god."[13] Sexual integrity means that we work toward a beautiful sex life within marriage, but that we keep this pursuit in context.

If you think of great sex or a great marriage as the greatest goal and fulfillment of your life, this itself can become an idol. You will be filled with resentment and self-loathing when marriage ends up being less than you imagine it should be. Marriage is not your destiny. God is. This is why the apostle Paul, who understood the profound mystery of sex, so highly valued his status as a single Christian. In essence, he "skipped" the metaphor of marriage and went straight into total intimacy with Christ.[14]

Through redeeming your sex life, God has the greater goal of refining your love for Him. Don't become so focused on the temporary gift of sex that you lose sight of its eternal significance.

Here's the most frustrating and freeing aspect of sexual integrity. You will never one hundred percent arrive. There has never been a moment in which I have truly loved the Lord my God with all my heart, with all my soul and with all my strength. In the same way, there has never been a sexual encounter with my husband in which I have experienced the complete fullness of all that God designed sex to be. I have always brought with me to the bedroom some degree of wrong expectations, selfishness, and fear. And honestly, so have you. But God is redeeming and restoring our sexual relationship to become more and more a reflection of His covenant love. We are growing individually and together on our journey of sexual integrity.

Remember, integrity means . . .
> Inviting God into your sex life.

> Your sex life resembling the puzzle.

> Remembering that sex and marriage matter because they point to God's relationship with us.

Part 2

PILLARS
OF A GREAT
SEX LIFE

Chapter 4

Pillar 1—
Faithfulness

When I began writing this chapter, it felt too soon to dive into the topic of faithfulness. It's much more fun and appealing to write about the "sexier" topics first and deal with unfaithfulness as a special issue later. But I realized that no other aspect of sex will work correctly if we don't first establish the foundation of fidelity in marriage. The covenant of marriage offers unparalleled beauty and passion, but these gifts are impossible for a couple to experience without the promise of faithfulness.

If you and your spouse have never experienced sexual betrayal, you might be tempted to skip this chapter. I encourage you to keep reading. Although many married couples acknowledge that fidelity is key to a healthy marriage, few can articulate why. And most couples define sexual faithfulness as not sleeping with someone else. What you do with your body is the expression of what you value in your heart. Faithfulness is not as simple as avoiding adultery. It is the wholehearted commitment to establishing the atmosphere of trust.

WHY FAITHFULNESS MATTERS

One day in the busy blur of raising young children, I had gotten out of the shower and was picking out my clothes for the day. Lost in thought, I didn't realize that my four-year-old son had wandered into the room. I turned to find him staring at my naked body. In that moment of panic, I was trying to figure out how to get him out of my room without shaming him (or saying something that would one day ruin his honeymoon!). My son must have recognized the terror in my eyes because he said with great composure, "Mom, don't worry. I won't laugh."

The most important ingredient of sexual intimacy is character.

I've often reflected back on that cute childhood story. Sometimes our children utter wisdom in their innocence. My son, even at four years old, understood that nakedness means vulnerability.

Every aspect of sexual intimacy involves risk. To play together, to experience an orgasm with your spouse, to fail sexually, to reveal hidden thoughts and fears, to expose shame from the past, to work through wounds . . . it all carries the risk of being laughed at, abandoned, or rejected.

The most essential element of a great sex life is not a toned body, a beautiful face, sexual skills, or even the capacity to think erotically. The most important ingredient of sexual intimacy is character. Without the promise, "I will never leave you or reject you," you cannot be known, you cannot celebrate with abandon, and you cannot endure through the inevitable valleys. You might be able to get physically naked without trust, but true intimacy is impossible without it.

Earlier, I shared with you that our honeymoon experience was less than magical. After we had tried once again unsuccessfully to have intercourse, Mike and I were both disappointed, hurt, and angry. Mike went to his corner of our small log cabin, and I went to mine. I remember feeling lonely, discouraged, and helpless. About an hour later, I looked over at my husband and saw he was reading the Bible. He then walked toward me, hugged me, and said, "I know this is a discouraging way to start our sex life, but we have a lifetime to figure it out. I want you to know that I love you."

What my husband said to me in that vulnerable moment placed a brick in the foundation of our new marriage. He was disappointed and frustrated too. Yet, he chose to comfort me, remind me of his love, and assure me that he wasn't going anywhere. There have been many times throughout our marriage when we have needed to reaffirm this promise to one another.

As I mentioned earlier, faithfulness in marriage is more than the commitment to not sleep with someone else. It is the consistent choice to say, "I will always choose you." All of the sex manuals in the world cannot compensate for a lack of this kind of trust in your marriage. God intentionally designed sexual intimacy to be dependent upon faithfulness. Why? Remember. The physical picture of sexual intimacy in marriage points to the spiritual intimacy God designed us to have with Him.

Faithfulness is the cornerstone of our relationship with the Lord. Without trust in God, you could not grow in intimacy and your worship would be simply a shallow expression. You have to know that His heart is for you, He hasn't left or rejected you. He desires the best for you. Before ever asking us to be faithful to Him, God showed us His faithfulness. He initiated love, pursuing us even while we rebelled against Him. Many Christians have a superficial relationship with God because they don't trust Him. This is why the Bible is filled with promises of God's character:

> "For as high as the heavens are above the earth, so great is his love for those who fear him." (Ps. 103:11)

"Those who know your name trust in you, for you, LORD, have never forsaken those who seek you." (Ps. 9:10)

"Jesus Christ is the same yesterday and today and forever." (Heb. 13:8)

"For I am convinced that neither death nor life, neither angels nor demons, neither the present nor the future, nor any powers, neither height nor depth, nor anything else in all creation, will be able to separate us from the love of God that is in Christ Jesus our Lord." (Rom. 8:38–39)

When we trust God's faithfulness, we can put weight on that relationship, responding with our affection and surrender. God's faithfulness to us and His requirement for us to be faithful in response is expressed in the Bible through the concept of "holy jealousy."

UNDERSTANDING HOLY JEALOUSY

If I described you as "jealous," would you take that as a compliment?

Before you answer, consider this. God describes Himself as jealous. In fact, He calls Himself by the name Jealous:

Then the LORD said: "I am making a covenant with you. . . . Be careful not to make a treaty with those who live in the land where you are going, or they will be a snare among you. Break down their altars, smash their sacred stones and cut down their Asherah poles. Do not worship any other god, for the LORD, whose name is Jealous, is a jealous God." (Ex. 34:10, 12–14)

Our covenant marriage with God requires us to be faithful to Him and worship Him alone. God is jealous for His people. This may surprise you, but sex is most often used in the Bible in reference to this concept. Over and over again, God describes the idolatry of His people as prostitution, whoring, and a sexually unfaithful wife. When God's people cheated on Him, He expressed righteous anger. They had given away something precious that belonged exclusively to Him. God's love includes a holy jealousy for us.

In the book of Hosea, we find a clear example of how God is the most faithful of all husbands. The book tells the story of Hosea and his real-life marriage. The prophet's story serves as an allegory for how God pursues us and redeems us even after we have been unfaithful to Him. As Paul wrote to Timothy, "If we are faithless, he remains faithful, for he cannot disown himself" (2 Tim. 2:13).

If God's covenant love is the picture on the front of the puzzle box, then holy jealousy also has a place in every marriage covenant. There is a healthy jealousy between a husband and wife that builds the trust necessary to experience true intimacy. In essence, God says to us, "Don't pretend to love Me with your lip service all the while giving your heart to the things of the world. Don't be lukewarm. Make a decision. Do you love Me or not?" God's jealousy expresses the invitation to be in an authentic relationship with Him.

This same thing applies to your marriage. Either you are committed to one another or you're not. Don't wear the ring and title while giving yourself to someone else. If you say you love your spouse, show it with your character. A man should feel jealous if his wife tries to capture the attention of other men. A woman should feel jealous if her husband shares intimately about their marriage with a female friend. It's normal and healthy to feel angry if your spouse looks at porn or fantasizes about another person. You belong exclusively to each other in your sexual relationship.

Within the promise of covenant, our love is expressed through faithfulness. Otherwise, the relationship is just a facade. A lack of healthy jealousy is a sign of artificial intimacy. When we don't have a healthy jealousy in marriage, we are essentially saying, "I choose not to care about intimacy with you. You are not worth fighting for."

Some people avoid healthy jealousy because they are afraid of the possessiveness and anger that unhealthy jealousy represents. One couple who began their marriage as an "open" marriage thought the lack of jealousy would give them more freedom and security. Although they were Christians, they bought into the cultural lie that having the freedom to be with other sexual partners would enhance their marriage rather than threaten it. Brooke explains:

Growing up, I watched many women around me in the church and within my close family experience jealousy. It made people frantic, stressed out; caused major arguments, distrust, and controlling, needy, displays of terrifying anger and insecurity . . . ultimately suffocating the relationships. A woman's worst fear is supposed to be cheating, porn, not feeling good enough, right? I learned that all jealousy was dangerous. Maybe it was easier to just not be jealous. If you're open to everything then nothing becomes threatening or hurtful. My husband and I could do and feel whatever we wanted and never have it create fear or insecurity.

So, when Dane and I got married I was perfectly okay with our open marriage. I didn't feel threatened by porn use, I didn't get territorial, I never felt like an affair was the worst thing that could ever happen. As long as I was his "#1," the one my husband would never abandon, I was fine. I thought his unfaithfulness didn't bother me because I was more secure in my marriage than most women. We both had addictions to porn and masturbation, had mutual fantasies, and seemed to be very comfortable with this arrangement.

For seven years, everything seemed fine. But then everything changed. I experienced jealousy the way I'd always feared from the person I had been the most honest and upfront with. It shocked me so deeply that I felt our whole marriage and my relationship with him had been a lie. Things were obviously not as okay as we thought.

On the edge of despair and headed toward divorce, Brooke and Dane began the hard work of restoring their marriage. They spent two years in counseling, going through studies with mentors who helped them understand and live by God's design for their marriage and sex life. Brooke explains how her view of faithfulness and jealousy in marriage has changed:

Now I see how the wrong expression of jealousy can be destructive but so can the lack of the right kind of jealousy. Healthy jealousy makes me feel like I belong to my husband and am worth fighting for. By protecting myself from rejection, I was keeping myself from true intimacy.

I'm also learning the beauty of healthy jealousy for Dane. I've started to have moments when I am protective over his gaze, hoping that he never finds someone else to suit him better. I'm jealous over what his eyes are watching on his phone, jealous over how his sexual needs are getting met, and experience hurt when he admits that he's relapsed. My insides still HATE caring about any of these things; it scares me that I actually care!

It's scary to feel even holy covenant jealousy because jealousy always means the risk of being hurt. Being hurt if I wasn't heard or cherished. Hurt if he didn't guard his eyes from something that made me feel insecure and replaceable. Hurt if he someday did let his heart wander. Hurt if he didn't hold up his end of the marriage covenant. I believe these are things that are now pushing me toward more intimate trust and openness with Dane. I have to allow myself to feel "at risk" instead of avoiding the risk by compromising God's design for a marriage covenant. Healthy jealousy can provide security, belonging, and protection. These are the things I long for and am beginning to experience as we grow together!

Friend, the cornerstone of covenant is faithfulness to your promise. A marriage simply cannot work without that foundation. I don't know the exact vows you said when you got married, but I hope that they echoed the promise of God's faithfulness, "I will never leave you nor forsake you" (Heb. 13:5 ESV).

THE PARAMETERS OF HEALTHY JEALOUSY

As you read this, you may have alarm bells going off inside your head. Even within marriage, jealousy can be a destructive and even abusive quality. Not all jealousy between a husband and wife is good. While healthy jealous protects the relationship, unhealthy jealousy strangles intimacy.

If you'd met them in a small group, you would probably think that Brian and Abby have a wonderful marriage. His arm is always around her, his fingers tenderly running through her hair as they sit together. If you got to really know them, you would see a different story. You might hear about the argument they had last night because another man looked at Abby just a little too long. Abby might tell you how isolated she feels because of her husband's jealousy and constant suspicion. He insists on approving her friends, checking her text messages, and setting limits on how often she sees her family.

Unhealthy jealousy is not an exclusively male trait. A wife might immediately assume her husband is texting another woman or looking at porn any time he picks up his phone. She might grill him about female coworkers and become paranoid that he is criticizing her whenever he gets together with his friends.

If you experienced the trauma of betrayal in a previous marriage, this may understandably make you very sensitive to any reminders or triggers of your past relationship. Childhood wounds and past betrayals can predispose us to a posture of "you are guilty until proven innocent." This kind of jealousy strangles intimacy, even if the intent is to protect it. When the marriage vows have been broken in significant ways (like infidelity, continual lying, or pornography use), trust not only needs to be built, but rebuilt. The process of working through betrayal is a difficult one that will include more accountability for the spouse who has broken trust. However, in general, here are some important distinctions of healthy jealousy in your marriage.

Healthy jealousy reflects what is exclusively promised.

"Love the Lord your God with all your heart and with all your soul and with all your mind."[1] God's claim on me is absolute and total. This means that His jealousy for me is extensive. He can rightfully be jealous of how I spend my money, what I watch on Netflix, and what I think about. In fact, God can even be jealous of my love for my husband and children if it is greater than my love for Him.[2] God is my Creator, my Lord, and my Savior. His possession of me is not some cruel bondage, but reflects His rightful place as the One who spoke me into being and created me for Himself.

My husband and I have just an echo of healthy jealousy; we don't have a total claim on one another. For us to understand healthy jealousy, we must go back to what a healthy marriage promises. I haven't promised to live exclusively for my husband, nor for him to live exclusively for me. We don't own one another. Instead, we promised to share the exclusive bond of husband and wife with each other. There is a promise of intimacy that no one else is to share.

Mike's love for me and mine for him must have a clear distinction of the exclusivity God has called us to, while also giving a lot of room to walk out the other callings God has placed on our lives. God calls me not only to be a wife, but a mother, a sister, a friend, a minister of the gospel, a daughter, and many other roles. Healthy jealousy means that my husband understands that I first and foremost belong to God. There are times when we say no to spending time together so that one of us can minister to a hurting relative, invest in other friendships, and accomplish the work we have in a busy season.

Healthy jealousy in marriage means that both Mike and I have close friendships and other interests that we may not share together. However, those relationships don't threaten our exclusive marriage bond. In fact, we choose to be with people who honor marriage and who will encourage us to love each other well.

Unhealthy jealousy will draw boundaries that are inappropriate and unwarranted, squeezing away the freedom for one or both people to fulfill the many roles God calls them to walk out.

I love how Jannette describes what she learned about holy jealousy:

The word jealousy itself in our cultural context carries a negative connotation, so much so that it almost seems sacrilegious to place the word jealous next to the name of God. However, God Himself said He is a jealous God. This prompted me to look at the word jealous as it is used in the Bible for both God and man. I thought for sure that the root word of jealousy would be different when related to God as opposed to man. To my surprise it's the same exact word! Zeal or zealous. Synonyms include fervent and burning desire. In the Old Testament God was zealous/fervent FOR His people whereas in the New Testament man was zealous/fervent AGAINST the other. I realized that being jealous is about an intense state (being fervent or burning with desire) FOR something/someone or AGAINST something/someone. Looking at it through this biblical definition helps me understand that we should all be jealous (fervent, burn with desire) FOR our marriages. Jealousy goes wrong when we are fervently (or burn with ill desire) AGAINST one another.

Healthy jealousy promotes growing character and trust.

The goal of healthy jealousy is always to build trust. If you don't trust your spouse, how can you get to the point where that could change? Demanding boundaries will always squash trust rather than build it.

Unhealthy jealousy can move into extreme measures of control and become abusive. When one spouse refuses to trust the other with money, friendships, or family relationships, they cannot move into intimacy. All of the checking and restrictions in the world won't compensate for that lack of trust. In fact, the more you set restrictive boundaries, the less likely you will be to trust your spouse. Your demands just reinforce the belief that your spouse can't be trusted on their own.

> **Boundaries are most healthy when you set them for yourself because you want to grow in trustworthiness. They're rarely helpful when you set boundaries for your spouse.**

Instead, healthy jealousy looks at the source of the distrust. Has your spouse proven to be unfaithful in the past? Is there betrayal and wounds that haven't been addressed? Or does your lack of trust come from your own insecurity and baggage?

Boundaries are most healthy when you lovingly set them for yourself because you want to grow in trustworthiness. They're rarely helpful when you set boundaries for your spouse.

As you build (or rebuild) trust in your marriage, it's helpful to have conversations about what boundaries help you feel safe. You might make a request like, "I would like to have filtering software on all of our devices," or "I would prefer that you not travel alone with a female coworker." These are requests, not demands.

If you don't trust your spouse to implement healthy boundaries and honor reasonable requests, reach out to a counselor who can help you get to the root of what's going on. Both you and your spouse have to *choose* to be trustworthy. Becoming more insistent or controlling with boundaries isn't going to help with that.

Brooke's husband, Dane, describes what he learned about the difference between healthy and unhealthy jealousy:

> My jealousy was bound to catch up with me. God never intended for us to have an open marriage. It was years later that I learned the difference between destructive jealousy and the healthy kind I was meant to have for Brooke. My expression of jealousy became unhealthy when it was about my desire for control, which made our marriage feel unsafe for Brooke. Healthy jealousy doesn't push your spouse away, but instead it can draw them in. Unhealthy jealousy is laced with fear but healthy jealousy is secure. Where unhealthy jealousy is possessive and controlling, healthy jealousy is protective and inviting.

WHY WE FIND FAITHFULNESS SO DIFFICULT

If we agree that faithfulness is such a cornerstone of a great sex life, why is it also a great challenge for most couples? I've met with both men and women who say things like, "I love my spouse. I don't know how I ended up having an affair!" or "I've tried everything I know of to stop. There must be something fundamentally wrong with me."

Sin always presents an illegitimate way to meet legitimate needs and desires.

Sin always presents an illegitimate way to meet legitimate needs and desires. Through sexual temptation, Satan offers us shortcuts to numb our pain, to feel alive, and to experience what we mistake as love. When we peel back the layers, we find that faithfulness is so difficult for a few key reasons.

You will have unmet needs and desires in your marriage.

In his book *Counterfeit Gods,* Tim Keller explains that the good gifts God has given us can become idols in our hearts. Sex and romantic love are among the most common forms of idolatry, even within the Christian church. In an effort to highlight the beauty and importance of marriage, this wonderful gift has become somewhat of an "acceptable" idol, or replacement for God's place in our lives. Keller writes, "Romantic love is an object of enormous power for the human heart and imagination, and therefore can excessively dominate our lives."[3] Even well-meaning Christian teaching can position marriage as the solution to all of your loneliness, sexual desire, and insecurity.

While marriage is a great gift, it is not the ultimate fulfillment, even for your sexual desires and temptations. You *will* be disappointed in marriage. You *will* experience lonely nights and longings that your spouse may not understand. This means that you *will* be tempted to find love, sexual excitement, or affirmation somewhere other than your marriage. There *will* be someone who is more attentive, understanding, or sexually arousing. You can count on it. When you encounter these temptations, remember the enemy's battle plan. He will wave something or someone shiny in front of you, telling you that you need this, you deserve this, and that this will bring you life. When this begins to happen, remember the adage: The grass is greenest wherever you water it! Invest in your real-life marriage rather than an illusion of something sweeter.

Sex is often used to meet underlying needs.

In many cases, sex is not just about sex.

Tara's home life was nothing short of chaotic. Her mom and dad both worked full-time, leaving her alone with siblings who were slightly older. When she was ten years old, her brother introduced her to pornography. This began a pattern of fantasy, pornography, and masturbation. When she was stressed, lonely, or depressed, sex helped her relax. Tara hoped that the love and sex she experienced in marriage would take away her temptations, and for a while, it did. But there were more and more days when she needed a sexual release and her husband wasn't interested.

Tara learned at a young age to use sex to self-soothe. Even within her marriage, sex was more about the physical release of stress than about connecting intimately with her husband.

Sex itself is not a need. Yes, there are drives and desires that can feel very much like a need, but you will not die without sex. We experience sex as a true need only when we pair it with other needs. Tara needed an escape for her constant anxiety. Sex was her "go to" road to rest. Others pair sex with love. Being physically embraced is the only way they can experience feeling needed, wanted, and appreciated.

We can use sex even within the confines of marriage to meet needs that have become attached to sex. So when sex is absent or unfulfilling, Satan offers other sexual outlets to "scratch the itch" of the deeper need.

You confuse sexual excitement for love.

Do you know that your brain releases a different chemical "cocktail" depending upon what kind of sex you have?

When you have new and exciting sexual or romantic experiences, your brain releases a combination of dopamine, adrenaline, and phenylethylamine. This combination of brain chemicals is designed to be a landmark experience, cementing images and sensations in your memory. Some say that this combination is actually more addictive than crack cocaine, inviting you to return again and again to the source of such ecstatic pleasure.

Imagine that you had this experience on your honeymoon, the

first time you and your spouse saw each other naked and touched each other sexually. In a perfect world, this would be your inaugural sexual experience. No pornography or images from things you've seen or experienced in the past. God gives a husband and wife this intoxicating and addictive experience to bond them together, inviting them to return again and again to one another!

When you have sex with your spouse over the years, you don't often re-experience this same sexual euphoria. Instead, your brain produces a different cocktail of hormones and chemicals. This type of sex releases bonding agents like oxytocin, vasopressin, and endorphins. These chemicals and hormones are designed to make you and your spouse feel close to each other and promote a general sense of peace and well-being. While this type of intimacy isn't the "fireworks" of honeymoon sex, it has huge benefits for relational bonding, trust, relaxation, stress relief, and even boosting your immunity.[4]

The impact of this increased oxytocin is particularly powerful for men in a committed relationship.

> In general, levels of oxytocin are lower in men, except after orgasm, where they are raised more than 500 percent. . . . This may also be why men are more likely to talk and feel emotionally connected after sex. In addition, there is an amnesiac effect created by oxytocin during sex and orgasm that blocks negative memories people have about each other for a period of time.[5]

Are you getting this? God is a genius! Sexual desire keeps us returning to a behavior that literally makes life together sweeter and more rewarding. The problem is that we can easily mistake a new sexual attraction as "true love" compared to the steadiness of consistent love. Marriage counselors note that "a lot of unnecessary divorces and relationship breakups can occur (when the infatuation stage wears off) because people mistake the lack of intensity and euphoria as a sign that they have fallen out of love."[6]

This is why it is helpful to be playful and creative and invest in your sex life. It also helps explain the draw to other sexual outlets like extramarital hookups or pornography. Porn hijacks the reward center of the brain and gives you endless options for novel sexual experiences. You get hooked on the dopamine, adrenaline, and phenylethylamine cocktail that simulates new love. Compared to the never-ending honeymoon high of porn, sex with your spouse can feel painfully dull and unsatisfying.

Fortunately, your brain has the capacity to be rewired in a way that builds true intimacy with your spouse. An article on the website "Fight the New Drug" reports on some research of the research explaining this:

> One of the main parts of your brain that is affected by porn use is the reward center. Basically what happens is that when this center gets overused, which results in it producing less of the "happy chemicals" (dopamine, serotonin, adrenaline, etc.) and also becoming less responsive to them. This means it takes more stimulation to make us feel good. If we eliminate porn as our main source of these chemical releases, our brain will start looking for new ones.
>
> We need start to connecting to positive things in our life that will actually support our physical, emotional, mental and social health. These connections might start off small, but they will grow and eventually replace the old neural pathways.[7]

3 STEPS TO BUILD TRUST

On your wedding day, you said vows. There is a good chance that you were too naive to even understand what you promised. "For better or worse, richer or poorer, in sickness and in health . . ." You vowed to love faithfully. If we are honest, we have all failed in the standard of perfect fidelity. You may have never cheated on your spouse, but have you fantasized about having sex with someone else? Have you ever wondered if you should have married another person or wished your spouse was more like . . . ? Have you ever withdrawn your love and affection because your spouse hasn't lived up to your expectations?

This is not intended to minimize the consequences of sexual betrayal. There is a big difference between thinking about an old boyfriend and sleeping with him. Something dies with infidelity. The magnitude of what happens in the wake of betrayal in a marriage speaks to the holiness of the covenant of marriage. This is why sexual unfaithfulness is one of the few reasons why God permitted divorce.[8]

Many, many couples have overcome and rebuilt intimacy after betrayal. They often say, "I'd never want to go through that again, but what we have now is far better than what we had before the infidelity."

Recovering from betrayal requires true repentance and forgiveness, and for both people to do the work of grieving and rebuilding trust. This is not a quick journey, and there are no shortcuts. If this is your story, I urge you to seek help from a counselor who can help you in the process. You may also find specific help from books like *Torn Asunder* by David Carder, *Faithful and True* by Mark Laser, and *Fight for Love* by Rosie Makinney.

Although most couples will not experience infidelity, they will all walk through imperfect love and fail one another. None of us are perfectly trustworthy, nor do any of us have a jealousy that isn't in some ways clouded by our own insecurities and fears. Faithfulness is a commitment of character. It is a journey of learning to love beyond what feels good in the moment. Healthy couples accept this journey, knowing that failures of faithfulness come in all different forms. If you want to walk forward in that journey, here are three things you can do:

1. Tell the truth.

By telling the truth, I don't mean thoughtlessly telling your spouse every way they have ever disappointed you. That's just cruelty. As Paul wrote, we should "speak the truth with love."[9] Our words should be seasoned with grace and sensitivity. What I'm referring to is the refusal to keep secrets from one another.

We will learn to be either sin concealers or sin confessors. Unfaithfulness doesn't begin with an affair. It starts with the secret temptations, thoughts, and wounds we hide in marriage.

Stop hiding. Stop pretending, even with the excuse of sparing your spouse's feelings. I'm not suggesting that you share every fleeting thought or temptation with your spouse. It is not your spouse's job to make you feel better about what you've done nor to keep you accountable. You need some trusted, same-gendered friends or a counselor to ask you the hard questions and to serve as a "safe place" to talk through the details of temptations and failures. But be willing to honestly and lovingly talk with your spouse about the gaps you feel between you, to confess your failures, and to express your desire to become a trustworthy person.

2. Make a new commitment.

The most important thing about you is what you choose. Not how you feel, not what you've done in the past, but who you resolve to become. Author Gary Thomas challenges husbands from his own journey of faithfulness:

> Do you think you could pray this week, "God, let me start looking at my wife like Adam looked at Eve—as the only woman in the world?" It's a prayer first, then a choice, then a recommitment. You will stumble. You will have to go back and pray again. You will have to choose again.
>
> But if you keep doing it, eventually, it happens.

Your wife is cherished.

Your wife isn't just your first choice, but your *only* choice.

You become happy, satisfied, and fulfilled.

Because your wife defines beauty for you, your picture of the most beautiful woman in the world ages with your wife. You won't be a sixty-year-old man pining after a 25-year-old centerfold. Who wants to be that guy, anyway?

You'll eventually be a sixty-year-old husband who is enthralled with his sixty-year-old wife and still finds his heart skipping a beat when she smiles in her own particular way, or she stands in front of you in that dress and the sun hits her just right and you forget about everything else, including time.[10]

Gary's wisdom is true not just for men, but also for women. We become what we choose. Every day, God gives us the opportunity to make a new choice. Will you choose to be a man or woman of faithfulness?

If your answer is "yes" put a stake in the ground. Tell your spouse. Tell the Lord. Renew your vows. Do something to say, "From this day forward . . ." And then, choose again and again to become a man or woman who is faithful and trustworthy.

3. Say yes to discipleship.

Walking out true faithfulness in your marriage begins with a commitment, but it certainly doesn't end there. Faithfulness is the fruit of the outgrowth of the character God wants to develop in you. This requires discipleship. You can find books that will tell you exactly where to draw boundaries with coworkers and how to set up hedges in your marriage. While this is helpful advice, it doesn't get to the root issue of character and how the enemy so skillfully lures us into temptation. Rules are necessary because we lack the discernment to see where our character is weak.

Like any other aspect of life, Christlike character grows as we intentionally pursue spiritual maturity. Building character is like building muscle. We must be willing to be broken down and then built back up.

God created you to spiritually be nurtured by spending time with Him and through learning from the mature people around you. I am so thankful that you picked up this book because this is a piece of discipleship! But you also need imperfect, mature people of God to encourage you and mentor you as you strive together to live out the faithfulness God has called you to.

Friend, regardless of where your marriage has been, God wants to teach you the beauty of His committed love. Accept His invitation not only to be faithful to one another, but to respond to His faithfulness with a wholehearted devotion to Him. This will truly set the stage for the other pillars of covenant love in your marriage.

Chapter 5

Pillar 2 —
Intimate Knowing

Over the past several decades, sociologists and psychologists have noted that the meaning of sex has dramatically changed. Two naked bodies no longer signal intimacy and commitment, but rather a momentary coupling or negotiated social exchange. My bookshelf is lined with books from secular researchers raising concerns about hookup culture and cheap sex and even decrying the "end of sex" as we know it. Smartphone apps and anonymous websites make millions of dollars by facilitating sex without meaning. No strings attached. The world of virtual reality will soon provide graphic sexual experiences with absolutely no human contact.

While the harm of such thoughtless sex outside of a committed relationship may be obvious to you, I'd encourage you to consider whether sex in your marriage is also void of meaning. Just because you are married doesn't mean that sex will automatically become a vehicle for intimacy. For some couples, sex is just a sanctified hookup. A husband and wife share their bodies, but little else.

Maria described that experience this way: "I know Joe loves me but when we have sex I just feel like an object to satisfy him. I wonder if he would be just as happy having sex with some random woman." Sean said it like this: "Whenever we have sex, I feel like my wife isn't really there. She gives me her body, but it's like her mind is a million miles away. I can tell she's not into it. Even though she is trying to meet my needs, something about it just feels unsatisfying."

I'm not referring to casual, quick, and fun sex that happens within marriage. Even "quickies" can be part of the journey of sexual intimacy. Instead, I'm referring to the pattern of confusing sexual *activity* for sexual *intimacy*. You can be sexually active with your spouse for decades without ever experiencing sexual intimacy.

> **Sex was never designed to be obligatory, but to be the greatest invitation and expression of intimacy.**

"Hooking up" in marriage is far more common than we realize. This trend is reinforced not only by the secular culture but also by simplistic teaching in the church. The focus is on whether or not we are fulfilling a sexual obligation. Sex was never designed to be obligatory, but to be the greatest invitation and expression of intimacy.

Sex without intimacy is perhaps the sneakiest counterfeit in marriage, gutting the gift of sexual intimacy of its true joy and significance. Like every aspect of sexual intimacy, we need to go back to the front of the puzzle box to expose this counterfeit and embrace what healthy sex is meant to look like.

THE SECRET OF *YADA*

Several years ago, my friend, author Dannah Gresh, showed me something in the Scriptures that has transformed my understanding of God's design for sex. It's all wrapped up in the word *yada*. *Yada* is the Hebrew word for sex often used in the Old Testament. "Adam *yada* Eve and she conceived."[1] This word *yada* means "to intimately know." The Old Testament also uses more casual words for sex like *bow* (this means to enter into) and *shakab* (which means to lie with).[2] While *bow* and *shakab* describe the physical act of sex, *yada* communicates that sexual intimacy involves a deep knowing of one another.

This Hebrew word *yada* is used over 940 times in the Old Testament. It is often used in reference to how God intimately knows His people and their longing to intimately know Him. *Yada* is not just intellectual knowledge, but a deep, experiential knowing. The intentional double use of this word in the Old Testament should catch our attention. God wants to *know* us as intimately as a husband and wife can sexually *know* one another. It's not that God wants to have sex with us, but that sex is a metaphor of how intimately God wants to be connected to us. He wants to know us like a man knows his wife when she is most vulnerable.

Moses had a very intimate relationship with the Holy God. He spent forty days alone on a mountaintop, basking in the presence of the Almighty. This intimacy with God made him want more! He asked the Lord, "If you are pleased with me, teach me your ways so I may know you and continue to find favor with you."[3] You may remember that God answered this request by passing before Moses as he hid in the cleft of a rock. God spoke His personal name to Moses and had a depth of fellowship with him that no one else on earth had experienced.

David is another man who was known for his intimate relationship with God. The Psalms record David's personal journal, showing us how he cried out to God in good times and trials. Psalm 139 is often referred to as the Psalm of intimate knowing (or the Psalm of *yada*). This Hebrew word is used five times in the Psalm (paraphrased below):

You have searched me and *yada* me!
You *yada* when I sit down and when I rise up.

Before a word is on my tongue, you *yada* it completely.
Your works are wonderful; my soul *yadas* it very well.
Search me, O God, and *yada* my heart.

God intentionally inspired the same word for sexual intimacy as He used to describe the intimate experiential knowledge He desires to have with His covenant people. In the New Testament, this theme of intimate knowing continues. The night of the last supper, Jesus told His disciples to abide in Him like a branch is connected to a vine—absolutely inseparable. Over and over again, Paul pleaded with the early church to *know* the love of God through Jesus Christ. The entire message of the Bible is the call to *yada*!

Adam and Eve experienced perfect *yada* with each other and with God before sin entered the world. Then, everything changed. The first thing Adam and Eve did when they sinned was hide. They hid from God and from one another, blaming instead of embracing.

Yada became an elusive ache in the human soul, the deep longing to be known, embraced, celebrated, and naked without shame. *Yada*, either with God or your spouse, will never just happen. It has to be intentionally pursued at great cost. Instead, we often settle for the counterfeit. We become complacent with being partially known both with God and with one another.

ACTIVITY REPLACES INTIMACY

Both in our relationship with God and in our marriages, we can confuse *activity* with *intimacy*. Often our activity keeps us too busy to realize how much we lack intimacy. This has certainly been true in my own journey.

As a young child, I accepted Jesus Christ as my Savior. In high school, I embraced Him as my Lord. But it wasn't until I was forty years old that He became my intimate friend.

At the time, I was in vocational ministry, serving God faithfully, obeying the rules, and rarely missing my daily devotions. I was *that* Christian, in good standing with God because I was *doing* all of the right things. Then I met a woman whose life showed me there was more. She talked about God using phrases like "He's my Beloved. He's my best friend. God is so gracious and sweet to me." It wasn't just her vocabulary. Something about her presence displayed an intimacy with God I had never known.

I felt like I had spent decades outside the gates of God's presence, peering in at Him from time to time. I toiled and studied, learning more about Him and desperately wanting to please the Lord, but assumed intimacy was too much to hope for this side of heaven. But then I saw my friend sitting right there in the very presence of God! I thought, "How did she get there?"

That awareness began a journey to seek the heart of God like I never had before. If it were possible to know God so intimately, that's what I wanted. I had spent a life in the activities of Bible reading, serving, and obeying (which are all good!) but neglected the greater call to intimacy. It is possible to be surrounded by the things of God and never *yada* Him!

As I grew in deeper and deeper *yada* with God, I realized that I had been on a similar trajectory with my husband. Sex was all about the activity. How often should we be having sex? Was I pleasing my husband? Was I a good wife? What about all my physical flaws? For years, I had completely missed the deeper invitation to sexually know Mike and be deeply known by him—*yada*!

There were other compartments of our marriage in which Mike and I talked and shared vulnerably. We were good teammates and friends. But sex was different. We never shared openly about our sexual struggles, disappointments, desires, and longings. It's almost as if when sex was involved, we pressed pause on our friendship so our bodies could do what they were supposed to do. We were just too different sexually and sharing about things so personal and vulnerable was uncomfortable.

When I began to experience such deep intimacy with God, I also began to crave a deeper intimacy with Mike. I couldn't put it into words at the time, but something within me awakened. My heart wanted to love and be loved in ways that I'd never experienced before. I wanted sex to be more than duty or going through the motions. I wanted to connect intimately with my husband. I wanted *yada*.

This awakening to *yada* helped me see that all of the sexual challenges we had faced over many years of marriage were also invitations to intimate knowing. Could I share my insecurities with him? Could I strain to understand his perspective and experience without lashing out in anger? Could we talk about sexual temptation without the fear of rejection?

Our sex life has grown exponentially, not because we learned some new technique, but because we are embracing the secret of *yada*.

THE GREATEST CHALLENGE OF YOUR SEX LIFE

The greatest challenge to both your sex life and your relationship with God is to continually pursue *yada*. No matter how great your orgasms may or may not be, your sex life will plateau if you are not willing to enter into *yada*.

Sex without *yada* is like food without nutrition. God gave you the gift of sex not simply so that your body could experience pleasure, but so that the physical act of becoming one would usher in a deeper knowing and intimacy with one another.

But there is a problem: being known is terrifying! From the time we are little children, we realize there are parts of our bodies and more significantly, parts of our being that just are not acceptable. We learn to accentuate the good and hide the bad. We hide behind our accomplishments, busyness, and excuses. We adapt by presenting a version of ourselves we believe God and others will accept. The intimacy of marriage and sex, by design, invites you to more. Sex by its very nature calls for nakedness and vulnerability.

Unfortunately, we learn how to hide even while we are naked. We figure out how to give our bodies while dressed in the armor of emotional self-protection. We split off the bodily experience of sex from the reality of being intimately known. And then we wonder why sex feels more alienating than satisfying.

There is no such thing as risk-free *yada*. God Himself took a risk when He created us for *yada*. Repeatedly, we reject Him, reinvent Him, and ignore Him as He pursues us. We give Him lip service of love while living our lives exactly as we please. We perform our spiritual duties while our affections toward Him are ice-cold.

This is why the first pillar is so important. There can be no *yada* without the promise of faithfulness. To the extent that you have experienced broken trust in your relationship, this must be repaired to provide the safety to be known. The more you trust, the more you can *yada*. And the deeper you *yada*, the more you can trust.

Tosha and Jake's story describes this process of building trust and learning to be vulnerable in their marriage:

Tosha:

> Jake and I both grew up in legalistic Christian homes. You kept your sin struggles a secret as you worked privately to figure them out. It felt shameful to even admit being tempted. As a result, I learned to hide unacceptable thoughts and temptations.
>
> I also learned that it was my job to make sure that men didn't fall sexually. The message was that men were created with lustful desires they could not control and it was the women's responsibility to make sure men stayed under control. Hearing this as a young woman began to harden my heart against men,

including spiritual leaders. I saw them as out-of-control creatures who would not take responsibility for their own thoughts and actions. I lost all respect for men.

Then I met Jake. He was athletic, handsome, funny, and loved Jesus. What more could I want? We were best friends first, and I felt like I truly knew him.

We went into marriage with little counseling because we were a "godly" couple so we didn't really need it, right? We jumped right into ministry, looking and acting the perfect part. We knew it was all an act. We needed help. When we approached one of the pastors for counseling, he basically said, "You are in ministry, you can't have problems" and handed us a book to read. My husband knew enough about my fears of men to hide his struggles with porn and lust. I had a sense that Jake was hiding something from me. I began to accept that he was just like every other man. I couldn't trust him, and I was crushed.

This unspoken issue became a huge wedge of guilt and resentment in our marriage. We felt like strangers living together. I felt lost and alone. Then God began to peel back layers and reveal to me my bitterness and pride. I knew my husband had his own struggles, and I knew he was too afraid to be real with me.

One night, during a long road trip Jake took the first step toward vulnerability.

Jake:

I remember feeling like this was a "make it or break it" moment in our marriage, and I honestly wasn't sure how it was going to go. All I knew is that the step I was taking was the right one. I had peace about that. The reality was that it only could go a couple directions: either we were going to have a marriage that appeared fine but was actually fake or we were going to have a marriage that appeared messy but was actually healthy. If I was willing to share the ugly parts of my heart (lust, pornography, self-idolatry, allowing other females to capture my attention, etc.), it would please God. I had to get to a point where pleasing God was more important than protecting my version of our "healthy looking" marriage.

Tosha:

As Jake cried and poured out his heart to me, God began breaking my hardened heart and gave me love for this broken man. God started to show me that my sin was just as dark and ugly and I needed His grace as much as anyone.

We were two hurting people who God brought together. I have told Jake since then the thing that truly got to my heart was not only his vulnerability but also his willingness to own his struggles. Not one time in our conversation did he ever try to blame me or make me feel responsible for his struggles. God allowed me to see the weight of the shame Jake had carried alone for so many years. That night, God gave us hope that He could restore our marriage and help us truly become "one." We haven't stopped that journey. Once we got a taste of true intimacy, we never turned back.

Jake and Tosha had a breakthrough in their relationship that invited them to be vulnerable with one another. This changed everything in their marriage and began a journey of intimate knowing.

THE JOURNEY OF INTIMATE KNOWING

Sexual activity will always focus on the event. Was the sex good? Did you climax? Is your body arousing? How did you perform? Are we following the rules? Sexual intimacy, instead, focuses on the journey. Ironically, it is often in the seasons when sexual activity isn't going so well that opportunities to know each other more intimately present themselves. Which is more intimate? Having sex or . . .

- Confessing to your spouse that you looked at porn last night?
- Grieving together that another month went by without getting pregnant?
- Explaining how you feel like a failure because you couldn't get aroused?
- Describing what kind of sensation triggers memories of past sexual trauma?

These aspects of the sexual journey are far more intimate than simply the act of having sex. They require that you get naked emotionally.

The act of sex for most people comes somewhat naturally. The physical part may be clumsy or painful, but you can probably figure out how to insert a penis into a vagina. The invitation of intimacy is far more complicated and elusive. Remember, *yada* is a journey, not a destination.

Maybe you, like many other couples, have no idea how to move from sexual activity to sexual intimacy. You've approached sex the same way for so many years, it seems impossible to make the shift. Because sexual intimacy is a journey, all you have to do is take one step in the right direction. Then another, then another. Here are four ways you can shift the focus from sexual activity to *yada*.

Learn to talk about sex.

One very practical reason that couples don't move beyond sexual activity is because they don't have the vocabulary to do so. What words do you use? How do you initiate a conversation about such a personal topic? You can't communicate your fears, longings, and feelings if you can't put them into words.

We talk a lot about sex in our culture, but rarely modeling vulnerability and tenderness. That is why it may be helpful to let someone else go first. We live in a day where there are many helpful conferences, podcasts, studies, and books to help with practically every area of sexual intimacy. For example, listening to a couple describe how they recovered from an affair or how they navigated the aftermath of childhood sexual abuse will give you a framework for how to discuss these difficult conversations in your own relationship. Honest, God-centered resources can give you the language and model how to talk about sex in a way that builds rather than threatens intimacy. Even reading this book together can give you language and permission to describe what you have experienced but been unable to express.

I remember years ago when Mike and I attended a marriage conference that addressed sexual intimacy. It was a Family Life Weekend to Remember event, and sex therapists Cliff and Joyce Penner spoke. I don't remember anything specifically about what they said, but I remember their giving me the permission and words to communicate something I didn't know how to tell my husband. Mike and I also learned to read books together out loud to one another. This made it less awkward to name body parts and describe different aspects of sexual pleasure and response.

While someone else's words can be a starting point, it's also important for you to make your sex life your own. What words are *you* comfortable with? Be specific and intentional in building your own sexual vocabulary as a couple. You may be using slang or other expressions that trigger your spouse without even realizing it.

What verbal or nonverbal cues do you want to use to communicate . . .

Her anatomy (breasts, vagina, clitoris):

His anatomy (penis, testicles):

Climax:

I need to take a break for a minute:

I would like to have sex:

Now is not a good time:

I'm really into it:

I'd like to have sex, but I need _____:

Unpack the meaning of sex.

This book is giving you a context to understand the deeper purpose and meaning of sexual intimacy within your marriage. There is a universal meaning of sex built into God's design. However, the various aspects of sex also have very personal meaning for each one of us. You can't read about those in a book. You can only learn those by pursuing the heart of your spouse.

One of the most respected forerunners of conversations about Christian sexuality is psychologist Doug Rosenau. In addition to writing and training clinicians, Rosenau regularly works with couples who struggle with various aspects of sexual intimacy. In his work, he highlights the importance of understanding the meaning of sex for a husband and wife:

> Sex is always more than sex. In any endeavor in life, it can be invaluable to explore the deeper meaning of that activity. Couples can benefit from unpacking and discussing what they want their sex lives to mean and express in their marriage.[4]

Rosenau recommends that couples ask each other questions like:

- What does the frequency of our lovemaking mean to you as a lover?

- What do certain behaviors (like kissing, oral sex, caressing the penis or clitoris) mean to you?

- How would you verbally or nonverbally communicate feeling excitement? Pleasure? Intense desire? Affection?

- How does initiating and postponing sex affect your lovemaking?

- What does it mean to you when your spouse initiates sex? What keeps you from initiating sex with your spouse?

- What does it mean to you when your spouse postpones sex?

- What sexually makes you feel embarrassed, experience shame or become inhibited?[5]

These questions and conversations move sexual activity to sexual intimacy. Instead of having sex with a body, you begin experiencing the journey of love with your spouse. As you tackle questions like these, and the ones at the end of each chapter, you might quickly hit a wall that feels too intimate or vulnerable to share. Don't let this discourage you. Instead, let it motivate you to continue to take steps toward one another. Yada isn't built in a day or week or even a year. Over time, you slowly learn to reveal more of yourselves as you confront barriers, wounds and learn to put words to the powerful experience of sexual intimacy.

Connect your body with your presence.

Remember way back, when holding her hand set you on fire. Think of the first time he put his arm around your waist. Touch had electricity and meaning. Over time, we learn to experience touch in a way that is split off or disconnected from intimacy. We fall into ruts like "he touches here, she kisses there, and then they have sex." The body is acting out intimacy, but husband and wife are just going through the motions.

We move toward intimate knowing when we intentionally reconnect the experience of touch with its deeper meaning and sensations. Sex becomes less about intercourse or climax and more about discovery, safety, vulnerability, and experiencing one another.

The Penners describe a fifteen-minute exercise couples can do every day to build toward emotional, spiritual, and sexual intimacy:

- Connect emotionally by looking into each other's eyes. This boosts oxytocin, the trust hormone.

- Connect spiritually by sharing an inspirational reading or praying together.

- Connect physically by hugging for at least twenty seconds and kissing passionately for 5–30 seconds without leading to sex. This boosts oxytocin and dopamine.[6]

For many couples, this exercise is far more intimate than having sex. Just by investing fifteen minutes a day, you will be retraining your brain to pursue intimacy, not just sexual activity.

The disconnect of touch with your body may be even more pronounced if you have experienced sexual trauma. Traumatic experiences often result in dissociation, which is a sense of being disconnected from your body or feeling numb. While dissociation helped you survive a traumatic experience, it now interferes with your ability to feel present with your spouse. A trauma-informed therapist can help you identify triggers that cause you to dissociate, guide you in processing traumatic memories, and help you reconnect touch with your presence through exercises like sensate focus.

Have grace for the journey.

Sex is one area of marriage that often represents wounds and deep fears. Couples get stuck on the journey of sexual intimacy because they don't know how to talk about such sensitive topics. It's almost as if you are walking through a minefield, not knowing when a sexual conversation will step on shame, pain, or fear.

Laura described her frustration at not being able to talk about sex with her husband, Paul:

> Paul and I have had a passionate sex life for forty years. All of a sudden, he won't talk to me about it and shuts down every time I try to initiate with him. Paul has recently had trouble becoming aroused. I'm guessing this has something to do with his avoidance. But he's so sensitive about this, I know he won't talk about it. What should I do?

One husband explained what it feels like to be married to a wife who doesn't seem engaged in sex and won't discuss it.

> Sometimes when we are having sex, it's like Sara mentally leaves the room. I don't know what's happening, but she shuts down. I ask her what's wrong, but she won't talk to me about it.

Like these couples, you will hit a wall in sexual intimacy when there are locked doors sealing pain and shame. It may be tempting just to settle for sexual activity rather than do the hard work of building intimacy. Becoming vulnerable within such tender and wounded places means taking an incredible risk. You or your spouse might need time to process and express their experiences. Be patient. Be gracious. Be prayerful. Be willing to reach out for help.

The journey toward sexual intimacy will likely mean both of you venturing into areas of woundedness. Intimacy means vulnerability and emotional nakedness. It's a long process that can't be rushed. Sometimes, you will need to be patient. Other times, your spouse will need to support you as you heal. While you are waiting for your spouse to heal, God may invite you into your own journey of healing and discovery.

Charity explains how this process is unfolding as she and her husband intimacy in the wake of his sexual addiction.

My husband's addiction came to the surface in our third year of marriage. I never wanted to have sex again. I lost all drive sexually because it had brought me so much pain and hurt.

Once my husband stepped into recovery, I wanted him to be fixed. He was the problem. Then God began prompting me to look at my own brokenness. I started to wonder, "Do I have anything that needs healing? Where am I sexually broken? What is keeping us from full intimacy?" I had so much brokenness, shame, and pain from my childhood that I didn't realize I had brought into our marriage . . . wounds that resurfaced when I discovered my husband's addiction. Wounds I had buried.

- I was sexually molested by my mother's boyfriend repeatedly at age eight.

- My single mother had a lot of boyfriends that would come in and out of the house with her bedroom door always locked, and suddenly, we would happen to have our bills paid for with trips to Disneyland (she later confessed to me when I was in college that she sold her body to pay for our bills).

- My high school boyfriend was addicted to porn and made me watch it with him every time we hung out.

- I wore a purity ring as a freshman in high school, and students laughed at me and mocked me.

Sex takes two people willing to show up, be vulnerable, transparent, seen, known, and accepted. If I wanted to experience God's design for marriage and sex, I needed to heal from my deep wounds so I could show up and let go. To let my husband love all of me and every broken wound.

Sex has now become a journey for us to discover together. It is a place where we both get to show up broken yet seen and still loved. Being naked is, in essence, the most vulnerable act because it involves the risk of being loved and accepted or rejected and neglected. We were now on the journey of learning how much God loves us, forgiven us, and healed us. It is time for us to redefine our marriage bedroom together and take ground together.

Yada is a journey, not an event. It can take couples years, even decades, to develop the trust, the language, and the tools necessary to be so emotionally and physically intimate. When we pursue *yada,* sex becomes less about being physically naked and more about your willingness to expose your most vulnerable thoughts and feelings.

Perhaps begin with a prayer together:

Lord, we realize that much of our sex life has been more about activity than intimacy. Thank You for inviting us into more. Please show us the right next steps to take in order to yada *You and to* yada *each other. Give us the courage to say yes to your invitation to intimacy.*

Chapter 6

Pillar 3— Sacrificial Love

Our sons were seven, five, and one, and I was exhausted. In those days, I tried to get up before the boys so I could enjoy twenty minutes and a cup of coffee in peace. Then the day began. Running kids to school and activities, taking care of a baby, changing diapers, cooking, cleaning, and managing part-time work and ministry. By the end of the day, I was spent. When Mike and I put the kids to bed, I expected not to see them again until morning. I didn't have a lot of patience for, "I can't sleep. I had a nightmare. I'm hungry." Evening was my time.

Usually, I'd make a cup of tea, read a devotional, and maybe watch a show with Mike. I got in the habit of changing into my pajamas in the bathroom with the door closed because I didn't want Mike to initiate anything sexual. One night he said, "You look really tired. Would you like me to give you a back rub?" My response was, "What *kind* of a backrub?" In other words, *Is this an act of kindness or a prelude to inevitable sex?* I felt like I had given my body all day long. I was done.

No one, not even Mike, would describe me as a selfish person. In general, I wanted to meet the needs of the people around me. But I had a difficult time reconciling this with our sex life. I read books about marriage and attended conferences that encouraged me as a Christian wife to meet my husband's sexual needs. I was trying to do this, but it felt like a great burden. Honestly, having sex was right up there with, "I need to clean the shower or mold will start growing again." There was a subliminal fear that if I didn't give my husband sex, he might be tempted to cheat on me.

This pattern continued through many of the busy years of our raising children. One evening as I was doing my devotions, the Lord was calling me to deep places in my heart. I read in the Bible about Christ's followers denying themselves to take up their cross. Convicted, I prayed, "Lord, what has it cost me to follow You? How can I love You more deeply? I am willing to do whatever You ask me to." In this wrestling with the Lord, the Holy Spirit brought to mind my attitude about sex. He was prompting me to pray about our sex life, which I reluctantly began to do. Then He began prompting me to go to our bedroom and initiate sex with my husband.

I wrestled with God. In my heart, I was willing to go wherever God would lead. So why was I so hesitant to initiate sex? At that moment, a call to ministry in India sounded more doable than the ten-second walk to my bedroom. Why?

I eventually trudged up the stairs, walked into our bedroom, and said, "Do you know why I'm here?"

Mike gave me a playful look and replied, "Yeah, I know why you're here!"

I sheepishly shared, "I was praying, and it was like God told me to come up here and initiate sex with you."

"No way! I was praying, asking God to tell you to do that!"[1]

I think about this story often. There have been many times over the years when time with God has prompted me to love my husband, sexually or otherwise. But God's leading me to my bedroom that night was not just about initiating sex. I don't think God simply answered my husband's prayers by sending me upstairs. He had something greater in mind. God was inviting me on a journey of surrender and healing. I began to realize that my attitude, frustration, and perspective of sex had never been completely yielded to Him. Even my efforts to "meet my husband's needs" were more informed by duty and fear than love. God's design for sex is rooted in mutual self-sacrifice and mutual pleasure. No on had ever helped my husband and me see this greater picture.

In this chapter, I want to share probably the most surprising thing about the gift of sex. We view obstacles to pleasure, like mismatched sexual desire and physical limitations, as a great deterrent to what God created sex to be. At one level, that is true. It sure seems as if sex would be more fun and pleasurable if we could have exactly the same desire as our spouse. In fact, this is one of the reasons why Christian singles think it's good to have sex before marriage. "That's the only way we will know if we are sexually compatible!"

What we fail to recognize is that some degree of sexual incompatibility is actually "baked into the cake" of sexual intimacy. Only through the challenges of sex can we unveil and develop one of the four pillars of what it means to love one another as God loves us.

SEXUAL DIFFERENCES ARE PART OF GOD'S PLAN

As you read my opening story, chances are you related on some level. Maybe you are the one, like me, who has the lower desire in your marriage. Or perhaps you can identify with my husband's perspective. You got married expecting this desire to be fulfilled only to find yourself frustrated by a spouse who doesn't enjoy or crave sex the same way you do. Maybe you want to be adventurous but your spouse likes plain old vanilla sex every time. While your pain may run much deeper than navigating differences in marriage, let's start there. In his book *His Brain, Her Brain,* physician Walt Larimore describes some of the sexual differences between the genders:

- Men tend to be oriented physically; women tend to be oriented emotionally and relationally.

- Men are stimulated by images and sight; women are stimulated by feelings, smell, touch, and words.

- Men are quick to respond sexually and difficult to distract during sex; women are slower to respond and easier to distract.

- A man's orgasm is short, intense, physically oriented, and solitary; a woman's orgasm is slower, more intense, emotionally oriented, and (at least potentially) multiple.[2]

Add to these differences, men say they need sex to relax. Women say they need to relax in order to have sex. For men, sex is usually about the goal of climax, while women generally enjoy the tension of the journey. A man's sexual desire is based on a single constant hormone (testosterone) while a women's desire is based on several changing hormones. Men are also more likely to initiate sex while many women experience responsive sexual desire, getting "in the mood" only after they begin engaging sexually.

Gender stereotypes don't always fit. There are some couples who will say, "That doesn't describe us," and that's okay. These are sexual tendencies and patterns that often—but not always—result from the differences between being biologically male or female. Biological differences between men and women have existed since God created humanity as "male and female."

As you look over these differences, consider this: Do you think these gender differences existed in the garden of Eden before sin entered the world? Is it possible that Adam wanted sex with Eve and she said, "Let's go for a walk and talk first"?

Preston Sprinkle explains how God created women to be both similar and different from men:

> The Hebrew word translated "suitable" by the NIV is *kenegdo* and is only used here in the Old Testament (Genesis 2:18, 20). *Kenegdo* is somewhat difficult to translate into English, since it is a compound of the word made up of *ke*, which means "as" or "like," and *neged*, which means "opposite," "against," or "in front of." . . . Adam needed not just another human, but a different sort of human—a female.[3]

By God's design, men and women are similar, and also different.

Without a doubt, our selfishness and brokenness have made navigating our differences more complicated. Could it be that our sexual differences are not the problem, but actually expose a deeper problem? In our flesh, we only know how to love with selfish love.

Jesus told us that the most important thing we could do as His followers is to love God with all of our hearts and love each other with unselfish love.[4] God's greatest goal for us is that we become the best lovers. . . . that we follow the example of Jesus of laying down our lives for one another. As Christians, we kind of get that, but the principle seems to stop at our bedroom door. With sex, we assume the right to demand, withhold, and complain when we don't get our way. It's as if every other teaching about loving one another is suspended with sex. What's that all about?

IS SEX AN OBLIGATION OR RIGHT IN MARRIAGE?[5]

A man approached me after hearing me speak on the topic of sexual intimacy and thanked me for talking openly about such a sensitive subject. Then he began sharing his story. He had just divorced his wife of twenty-nine years because of a lack of fulfilling sex in their marriage. He explained that his wife didn't want the divorce, but that he saw it as an act of kindness. "Now we can both pursue someone who will meet our sexual need."

I've heard hundreds of stories like this. Christian men and women use Scripture to say that great sex is an essential right in marriage. One spouse forces another to have sex when and how they like because it's their "marital right." A spouse goes through decades of miserable sexual experiences because it's their "duty." Unfortunately, a lot of Christian teaching on sex has reinforced this thinking. The focus is on whether or not a couple fulfills a sexual obligation.

Does the Bible teach that great sex is a right in marriage? Some point to Corinthians 7:1–6 to the position that it does.

Let's take a look at what Paul wrote:

> Now for the matters you wrote about: "It is good for a man not to have sexual relations with a woman." But since sexual immorality is occurring, each man should have sexual relations with his own wife, and each woman with her own husband. The husband should fulfill his marital duty to his wife, and likewise the wife to her husband. The wife does not have authority over her own body but yields it to her husband. In the same way, the husband does not have authority over his own body but yields it to his wife. Do not deprive each other except perhaps by mutual consent and for a time, so that you may devote yourselves to prayer. Then come together again so that Satan will not tempt you because of your lack of self-control. I say this as a concession, not as a command. (1 Cor. 7:1–6)

As we walk through this passage, we need to remember two things:

1. This instruction is within the context of an ongoing discussion with the Corinthian church. This is why Paul quotes them. He is responding to something they asked, and we don't know the full context of this conversation. Notice that Paul also clarifies that this advice is a "concession" based on their current context.

2. This instruction is within the context of the entire Bible. When we build a theology of sex (or anything else) on a few isolated verses, we will often end up with a theology not representative of the entire message of the Bible. This is what I fear has happened in the case of these verses.

If you only read these verses to understand sex in marriage, you would probably conclude:

Sexual desire is a really bad thing. God made marriage to tame us sexually. That's why you have to give each other sex whenever one of you wants it. Otherwise, you (or your spouse) will fall into sexual sin. The only reason for denying your spouse sex is if you agree to have a period of prayer—and how long can a person really claim to be praying?

For much of the early years in my marriage, this is what I thought the Bible taught about marriage and sex. I heard sermons and marriage seminars essentially reinforcing this message. I was supposed to meet my husband's sexual needs because, if I didn't, he would be justified in cheating on me. This made me feel like a sex object to my husband. Although I knew Mike loved me, I still sometimes felt like physically I was being used for his pleasure based on a biblical teaching.

Oh, I wish that for those many years I had a more complete understanding of the beauty of God's gift of sexual intimacy! Here are a few things I wish I had learned about God's design for sex in marriage.

Sex is about mutual love.

The spirit of 1 Corinthians 7 is not to present sex in marriage as an obligation, but a call to take seriously the symbol of two lives united as one. Both the husband and the wife share their bodies with the other as a gift of love, symbolizing their lifelong promise. Notice that Paul emphasizes *both* the wife's and the husband's sexual needs. The call to meet your spouse's sexual needs does not just refer to the person who has the higher sexual desire. The lower desire spouse (whether it be the man or the woman) also has longings, feelings, and even fears that need care and attention. Unfortunately, most couples apply this passage only to the person who wants sex more and completely ignores the needs of the person who has to "give it."

If your sex life revolves around one of you, something is wrong. If your spouse rarely enjoys sex but engages in it just to keep you from temptation or to please you, your sex life is unhealthy and not in line with God's created design. In almost every marriage, one spouse will need to *nurture* the sexual desire of the other. This may include communication, counseling, patience, and learning to trust through non-sexual touch.

Most men and women who have a low sexual desire in marriage stay stuck in that place because they never take the time to explore and address barriers to intimacy. Mutual love calls us to consider the emotional, relational, and sexual needs of both the husband and the wife, no matter who expresses the desire for more sex. First Corinthians 7 is calling a couple to take seriously the journey of sexual intimacy, understanding that it has the power to unite or divide them.

Sex celebrates sacrificial love.

Let's say that we have a big anniversary coming up and I tell my husband, "Mike, I want to go to Hawaii for two weeks to celebrate our 25th anniversary." And what if Mike responds, "That's a nice thought, but we don't have the money for that kind of trip. And if we were to plan a trip like that, I'd much rather go to Europe."

In response to Mike, what if I said, "I don't care how much it costs. I don't care if you'd rather go to Europe. I don't care if we have to get a second mortgage on our home. I want you to take me to Hawaii for two weeks. I deserve this after twenty-five years of marriage!"

What's wrong with this picture? The purpose of an anniversary is to celebrate our love and to remember the vows we made and have kept. But in the planning of the celebration, my demands show a selfish, uncaring heart. If I acted like this, not only would we have a miserable trip, but my husband would likely be dreading the next twenty-five years of marriage!

The Bible clearly teaches that marriage and sex reflect Christ's love for His church. The act of sex should point to the unconditional love of Christ, not a selfish attitude that requires you satisfy my desires. Any man or woman who demands sex from a spouse has missed the whole point. Sex is a symbol of love. Demanding the symbol ironically obliterates the love sex was created to celebrate.

Later in the same letter to the Corinthians, Paul defines love as patient, kind, humble, unselfish, not easily angered, not holding grudges, protective, trusting, hopeful and enduring.[6] Is this kind of love supposed to be suspended at the bedroom door?

The celebration of covenant love means that both the husband and wife take steps to pursue actual oneness and unity. Both the spouse that demands and the one who withdraws get in the way of this pursuit of unity. Sacrificial love calls them both to work toward genuine intimacy, not just a sexual release.

Self-control is the work of the Holy Spirit.

It is also a terrible misinterpretation to think that Paul is blaming a wife for her husband's sexual sin (or vice versa) or putting pressure on her to meet his needs so he doesn't look at porn.

One young wife explains the devastating impact of this message:

I believed sex was my duty because of the advice a pastor gave us after sharing our sexual brokenness in marriage with him. I will never forget the words out of this pastor's mouth, "wear him out, girl." It had now become my duty to fulfill my husband and every desire he had so that he would not look at pornography. It led me to believe I was to fulfill his desires and if I didn't he would look elsewhere. Man, did this break my heart because it wasn't working. How could I become this perfect sex goddess for my husband? I felt so screwed up and believed I would never be good enough.

Not only is this advice devastating to the spouse who assumes a "duty," but it also keeps the struggling spouse from growing in Christian maturity. It's not marital sex that helps us control sexual temptations. As Paul taught in Galatians 5, it is only yielding to the Holy Spirit that can have that effect in our lives. Christian husbands and wives, under the power of the Holy Spirit, steward their sex lives for the greater purpose of covenant love.

> **The inability to steward your sexual urges, temptations, and desires is not a marriage problem, but a reflection of your lack of surrender to the Holy Spirit.**

Why do we expect Christian singles to have total self-control and denial sexually, and then assume within marriage we have the right to have every desire and fantasy met, even at the expense of the one we are called to love?

Whether you are single or married, self-control is a fruit of the Holy Spirit. The inability to steward your sexual urges, temptations, and desires is not a marriage problem, but a reflection of your lack of surrender to the Holy Spirit.

God's best for you is not a pain-free, blissful sex life. Great sex in marriage is a gift, but the greater gift is the character you must develop to love each other well, in season and out of season. God created sex in a way that will naturally stretch your capacity to love each other. Every challenge your sex life throws at you is an invitation to tangibly learn what it means to love as Jesus loves.

LEARNING FROM CHRIST'S LOVE

In 1978, before Hallmark Christmas movies were a thing, entertainer Marie Osmond starred in a film called *The Gift of Love.*[7] (I'm completely dating myself here!) I saw this movie once as a young girl and still I remember it. The film had all the elements of a classic romance story. Beth (played by Osmond) was from a wealthy family and was expected to marry a man her parents chose for her, but she fell in love with a poor immigrant, Rudi. When she and Rudi married, her parents cut Beth off financially. The couple didn't have two nickels to rub together.

The destitute newlyweds couldn't afford to buy each other Christmas presents. They each had only one possession that mattered to them. For Beth, it was her beautiful hair. Rudi's only treasure was a pocket watch passed down from his father. On Christmas morning, they exchanged gifts. Rudi had sold his precious watch to buy Beth an ornate, silver hair clip. Ironically, Beth cut her hair and sold it to buy her husband a gold chain for his watch. Although neither could use the gifts they received, the gift of love won the day.

Sacrifice is love's greatest expression. You will not find a truly romantic love story that doesn't echo the theme of love triumphing

over selfishness. Love means, "I love you more than I love myself."
Hollywood didn't invent this storyline. Great novels and movies only echo what is already written on our hearts: "Greater love has no one than this: to lay down one's life for one's friends" (John 15:13).

God's love for us required great sacrifice. Jesus came to earth, humbled Himself by taking on the form of human flesh, was obedient to everything the Father asked of Him and gave His life to save His beloved. In response, Jesus asks those who love Him to deny themselves and to lose their lives in pursuit of His kingdom. Christianity is built on this kind of self-giving love. Why are we surprised when the metaphor of sexual love within marriage costs us something?

The journey of sex transforms into intimacy when we recognize this: a great sex life is impossible without unselfishness and sacrifice.

The journey of sex transforms into intimacy when we recognize this: a great sex life is impossible without unselfishness and sacrifice. It may be as minor as sensitivity to your spouse's preferences and as profound as deeply loving a spouse who is physically or emotionally incapable of meeting your sexual desires. Choosing to serve your spouse sexually is not a duty, but the unfolding of a unique facet of Christ's love.

Before going any further, it's important to note a few things about sacrificial love within your sexual relationship.

Sacrificial love is always offered willingly, never taken or manipulated.

When Jesus predicted His death, He said, "I lay down my life for the sheep . . . No one takes it from me, but I lay it down of my own accord. I have authority to lay it down and authority to take it up again" (John 10:15, 18). Sacrificial love still has boundaries, as Jesus' love displays. He would not be manipulated or forced into complying with anyone's agenda. He willingly gave out of love for us and obedience to the Father. Our attitude toward one another should be the same.

Taking sexually from your spouse without their willingness is abuse. Using the Bible to manipulate your husband or wife or threatening to leave or cheat if you don't get your way is a gross distortion of Christ's love. Manipulated love or sex is not sacrificial love!

Ministry is not the same as intimacy.

First Corinthians 7 and other passages call us to the unselfish pursuit of intimacy. This is why Paul addresses *both* the husband and the wife equally.

The Message paraphase puts this in everyday wording that should resonate: "The marriage bed must be a place of mutuality—the husband seeking to satisfy his wife, the wife seeking to satisfy her husband. Marriage is not a place to 'stand up for your rights.' Marriage is a decision to serve the other, whether in bed or out."[8]

When one person in marriage becomes this kind of servant lover, marriage is ministry. When both people have this attitude, they enter into intimacy. There are seasons in marriage during which one spouse ministers to another sexually. However, intimacy doesn't grow until both the husband and wife begin to ask the question, "What does it look like to serve my spouse, both in bed and out?"

Jesus' life showed us both ministry and intimacy. Jesus not only gave, but He also received. He accepted Mary's lavish gift of worship even when some of His disciples criticized her.[9] He received the material provisions of women who cared for Him.[10] Jesus received the worship of the people crying out, "Hosanna! Blessed is he who comes in the name of the Lord!"[11] He asked His closest friends to be with Him during His time of trial and grief,[12] and He asks His followers to surrender their will to Him daily.[13]

To experience true intimacy, you must be willing to both give and receive. Sexual intimacy is impossible if one person's needs, desires, and longings are swallowed up by the other. Doug Rosenau explains it this way:

> Christians need to be able to practice both submission and a righteous selfishness [. . . .] We as Christians are indeed encouraged to be submissive. That is, we are encouraged to place our partner's needs and feelings ahead of our own. And submission is a significant part of a great sex life . . . But fulfilling sex also requires being selfish. If we are always other-focused or if we repress and ignore our own needs, we forfeit complete sexual fulfilment. Intimate lovemaking is a partnership with both selfishness and unselfishness.[14]

You might get tripped up on the word "selfishness" as it is used here, especially since much of this chapter is about the importance of unselfishness in marriage. Rosenau is saying that intimacy requires both the husband and the wife to be sensitive to the other's needs as well as *to their own needs*. One aspect of being great lovers is the joy of knowing that you bring your spouse sexual pleasure. If you are married to someone who will not or cannot articulate what brings them pleasure, this will diminish your joy. Sex is for intimacy, not only as a form of ministry.

Gary Thomas, author of *Married Sex*, shared with me on a podcast interview how thinking wrongly about sexual pleasure compromised sexual intimacy in his marriage, "As a young husband I was too focused on my wife's pleasure at the exclusion to my own." Gary explained that he heard so many stories about selfish husbands that he didn't want to be like that. Over the years, he learned that by suppressing his own pleasure he was not only withholding from himself, but also from his wife.[15] God created intimacy so that we get great joy out of bringing pleasure to one another!

WHEN PAIN RUNS DEEP

For some couples, sex represents pain far greater than basic gender differences. One man told me, "Nothing has tested our marriage more than the total lack of any sexual connection. My wife is attracted to women and experiences no sexual desire for me. That's not her fault, it's just the way it is. I understand that my calling is to love and accept her just as she is, just as God loves and accepts her. We are committed to our marriage and want to continue to work toward intimacy, but I still struggle with the feeling that for us both, our sexuality has been a curse and not a blessing, a source of frustration and disconnectedness and not of love and connection."

There are seasons of marriages where couples sacrificially abstain from sex to provide the room for healing and restoration such as when facing infertility or the loss of a child, lasting impact of childhood trauma, disabilities, disease, addition recovery, and mental illness. The passage in 1 Corinthians mentioned in this chapter refers to times when a husband and wife agree to not have sex so they can devote themselves to prayer. This type of sexual fasting and prayer may be necessary for couples to develop true sexual intimacy and for the brain to heal from the impact of trauma or addictive patterns.

While these difficult circumstances may compromise a couple's ability to enjoy the pleasure of sex, they also present the opportunity to grow in their understanding of sacrificial love. I have been humbled by couples who have walked through great difficulties together, leaning into the other pillars of sexual love even while regular sexual pleasure isn't their reality.

Sue described how her husband Mike's patience and gentleness have been such a pivotal part of her healing from past sexual abuse: "Mike has risked over and over again, patiently helping me on my healing journey. He has sacrificed and denied himself so many times when I could not meet his needs. And I had to sacrifice for his sake too. It was a huge risk to face my fears on the healing journey so that we could begin to experience true intimacy."

Charity explained what it has looked like for her to sacrificially love her husband through recovery from a sexual addiction:

When I first heard about the idea of celebrating covenant love, all I could think of were the vows we made on our wedding day and said to myself, how can we celebrate something that has been tainted and broken, filled with lies and deceit? I was first so sad when realizing our covenant was broken, but then it gave me a greater depiction of Christ's covenant with me. How many times have I broken His covenant with me? Yet, He still loves me and forgives me and pursues me and desires me. I broke our covenant with the Lord over and over and over again. Yet, He still celebrates me as His beloved daughter. This was so humbling.

On the journey of recovery, I am choosing to celebrate this newly restored covenant with my husband. It's a perspective shift from perfectionism to gospel-centered. I am celebrating how we are flawed and broken and sinners yet restored and mended and whole because of Jesus. That is what is now stamped on our marriage bedroom. We celebrate how far we have come, how God has cleansed us, how He has healed us, and now how we can choose to love one another because Christ first loved us.

Charity and Clint now run a ministry called Restored2More that helps couples recover intimacy after broken trust. Couples like these teach me through their choices to love each other well. God wants each of us to grow in our capacity to give and receive unselfish love.

Great lovers give freely out of what they have.

There are some things you can't give your spouse sexually. You don't have a perfect body, and your past may be scarred by wounds.

Emotional, relational, and physical poverty may make you feel like you have little to offer. More important than what you can give is this question: Are you a cheerful giver?

The Bible records a story of Jesus observing as people gave their offerings to the temple treasury. Some people made a great show of putting in big amounts of money. What caught Jesus' attention was a widow who gave a small amount, but it was all she had.[16]

What we give one another is often far less significant than the spirit from which we offer ourselves. Many of us silently or vocally apologize for what we can't give. *I'm sorry that I have so many wrinkles. I am ashamed that my body can't respond the way I wish it could. I wish I wasn't so fearful of touch.* Continually remembering what we can't give takes away the joy of what we can.

What does it look like for you to give generously to your spouse? Perhaps your gift right now is the commitment to the long journey of healing. Maybe intercourse isn't possible, but you lovingly find other ways to bless your spouse sexually. "God loves a cheerful giver" even when all we have to give feels painfully lacking.

Great lovers receive with grace and appreciation.

Our capacity to love with unselfish love is evident not only in how we give, but also in how we receive.

Gracious people are grateful for any gesture of kindness you offer. It doesn't matter what you bring them, they receive it as if it were a totally unexpected surprise. The opposite of gracious is a person who is never content with what you give them. Do you know anyone like that? You might search for days to give them a special birthday gift, and they subtly let you know that it's not exactly right. I don't know about you, but gracious people make me want to give even more for them. The opposite is also true. If I know I can't please someone, I just give up trying.

When your spouse offers you love, which are you more like?

The person who receives with gratitude or the one who complains or pouts because of what is lacking? Choosing to be a gracious lover can have a profound impact on the dynamic of your marriage.

> **Choosing to be a gracious lover can have a profound impact on the dynamic of your marriage.**

In every season of marriage, you can find ways to be disappointed in how your spouse falls short as a lover. You can also choose to be a gracious recipient of the good gifts you may be taking for granted.

As you read this chapter, you might feel overwhelmed with the idea of developing sacrificial love in your bedroom. Loving each other well is the result of learning to daily surrender to the power of the Holy Spirit in response to the goodness of God in our lives. God is so patient, so gracious, so forgiving, so generous to me. I want that love to overflow from my life onto my husband. This is a journey that takes time.

Decades ago, when God first asked me to go upstairs and initiate sex with my husband, the Holy Spirit's work wasn't about improving our sex life. Rather, He was prompting us to plumb the depths of genuine love.

There is perhaps no more tangible love lab than marriage. Feelings of love and natural attraction to each other can only get you so far. Rather than being depressed by that thought, be encouraged! God has a greater plan than sexual compatibility. He longs to form you into the greatest of lovers, in the image of His Son Jesus.

Chapter 7

Pillar 4— Passionate Celebration

I was sharing with my good friend, Yvette, about the message of this book. "I think it's unique because I'm unfolding how sex in marriage is a reflection of God's covenant love." You'd have to know Yvette to give context to her immediate response. She is the life of the party; all "7" on the Enneagram. She also loves Jesus and is one of my favorite people in the world.

"Juli, please don't make this book all 'imagine Jesus in the bedroom sitting on the bed.' Yes, He's everywhere, but that mental image is such a buzzkill. Please tell them sex is beautiful and sex is fun and sex is supposed to be hot. Sex is holy even without kneeling down to worship the Lord first!" (I told you she was fun!)

You get the tension here, right? If sexuality is a holy metaphor, does that mean we should play "How Great Thou Art" in the background every time we have sex? Should we use the King James verbiage when we talk about sex? "Wilt thou be willing to consecrate our marital covenant today?" Is there room for laughter, playfulness, unbridled passion, and red, hot pleasure within a Christian marriage?

Imagining Jesus sitting on the bed might be a comfort in some situations, but probably won't help the "fun" factor for most of us. There are many things God asks Christians to deny themselves. The pursuit of passionate, fun sex within marriage is not one of them. If *mutual* pleasure is not a part of your sex life, something is wrong.

Most of us fall to one extreme or the other on our perspective of sexual pleasure. For some, pleasure is the most important aspect of sex. They consider sex to be worthless if it isn't always physically fulfilling. Sex in marriage is not about the quest for the next sexual high. Sexual pleasure at the expense of the other three pillars (faithfulness, intimate knowing, and sacrificial love) will kill your marriage.

The other extreme is equally destructive: discounting sexual pleasure as sinful or at best, optional. Some Christians can't believe they have freedom, even permission, from God to enjoy sexual pleasure to the fullest. The enemy is diabolical in tempting us to experience sexual pleasure outside of covenant and then shaming us away from it within marriage. It's honestly a challenge for most of us to reconcile the holy nature of sex while also embracing sexual pleasure and ecstasy. At an unconscious level, we might even believe we are pleasing God by withholding or limiting the pleasure we experience. Gary Thomas explains it this way, "Religion tempts us to become more concerned with our pride-laced denial and self-exalting piety than bringing delight to our heavenly Father, who takes pleasure in our pleasure."[1]

Think about that statement. God takes pleasure in your pleasure. Do you believe that?

Parents go to great lengths to bring their children joy. They pick out special birthday presents. They treat them to their favorite ice cream. They plan elaborate vacations to the beach or an amusement park. If you have children, you've probably experienced both the glee of watching their enjoyment and the dejection when they mope rather than delight in what was meant to bring happiness. You know from a parent's perspective that being a "good kid" doesn't mean suppressing happiness and joy at the good gifts you give. Your child's delight brings you great pleasure. The same is true with God.

What do you think pleases the Lord more? A couple who goes through the routine of so-so sex or one that is playful, passionate, and unashamed in their pursuit of mutual, breathtaking pleasure? You are doing your heavenly Father no favors by limiting your experience of abandoned passion in your sex life.

Most people have to actively fight against roadblocks to pleasure, whether they be wrong attitudes about sex, memories from the past, or physical limitations. Sex may not currently be fun or pleasurable for you, but pursuing godly sex in your marriage means intentionally addressing barriers to mutual pleasure. Our culture's messages about sex present pleasure as if it will naturally happen. When a couple realizes that pleasure takes effort, this can be a major disappointment. Unfortunately, a lot of Christians resign themselves to a lackluster sex life because they don't perceive sexual pleasure as a worthy and God-honoring goal.

WHY YOUR PLEASURE IN SEX MATTERS TO GOD

Understanding the importance of celebration has helped me connect the dots of sacred sex and passionate pleasure. Every culture on earth makes space for the concept of "party." In biblical times, celebration was a huge part of the Jewish culture. In fact, God commanded them to observe regular feasts and parties as part of their worship. Their celebrations sometimes lasted weeks!

A celebration is a time set aside to enjoy people, food, and music. We throw parties both to remember significant events of the past and to rejoice in the victories of today. Because we value celebration, we invest time, money, and effort to make them fun and pleasurable.

God has given you as a married couple sexual intimacy as a way to regularly celebrate your covenant. Marriage has its share of hard work. In the midst of challenges, God gave the gift of sex to enjoy, play, and remember the beauty of your covenant to each other. Sex within marriage should be a regular party, remembering and celebrating the triumph of love over selfishness.

Tim Keller described sex as a "covenant renewal ceremony," celebrating with our bodies what we have promised to do with our whole lives.[2] God created sex to be a passionate, covenant celebration for two. Parties are supposed to be fun, joyful, playful, and full of expression. You don't go to a celebration to think or solve problems, but to experience joy. If the regular tone of sex in your marriage feels more like a visit to the dentist or a business meeting, you're missing out on what God created this gift to be.

When I asked Christian sex therapist Michael Sytsma about the place of sexual fasting for married couples, his answer surprised me. He noted that the Bible does talk about fasting but speaks far more often about feasting. Many Christians know how to practice sexual self-denial but don't know how to enter into the feast of sexual love in marriage.[3]

God takes pleasure in your sexual pleasure. How do we know this?

Look at the body.

God created everything about our bodies, including our capacity for sexual enjoyment. He crafted both the male and female genitals to be very sensitive to touch and wired with capacity for great pleasure. God created a man to be captivated by the sight of his naked wife. He filled a man's body with testosterone, prompting guys to think about sex and experience the regular desire for sexual release. That's a good thing!

And let's not forget how God created women. God crafted the clitoris with eight thousand nerve endings, almost twice as many as the penis. The clitoris has no other biological function other than pleasure. It's not part of reproduction or urination, like the penis. It has one purpose. "This tiny erogenous zone spreads the feeling to 15,000 other nerves in the pelvis which explains why it feels like your whole body is being taken over" during orgasm.[4] And speaking of orgasm, that was God's idea too!

When you have sex and experience orgasm, your body and brain join in your celebration as you are flooded with powerful chemicals like dopamine, oxytocin, and endorphins. Your body's natural response to sex is similar to the excitement, pleasure, euphoria, and peace you might experience when using drugs. Perhaps this is why Solomon gave the advice to be "intoxicated" by sexual love in marriage.[5]

Not only is the act of intercourse designed to be pleasurable, but God also created us to feel good when we simply touch one another. Back rubs, kissing, caressing each other, fondling your wife's breasts—while we often think of these activities as foreplay to intercourse, they are also ways that God designed us to experience the pleasure of intimacy even when touching doesn't lead to sex.

Our bodies have a profound natural capacity to experience great pleasure. While our culture looks for ways to exploit this gift, we need to remember that erotic pleasure is all part of God's creation. His created design should regularly remind us that the covenant celebration of sex can be like a sensual candlelit feast or an explosive dance party!

Look at the Bible.

If you ask the average person, "What does the Bible say about sex?" they will most likely highlight all the things God says no to. God is generally perceived as a killjoy in relation to sex.

The Bible is made up of sixty-six books. There is only one book among those that is specifically about a human relationship. Every other book is, in some way, about the relationship between God and His people. Only the Song of Solomon, also called Song of Songs, focuses on a human relationship. Note that the Song of Solomon is both literal and allegorical. In other words, it can be taken literally as a message to husbands and wives and can also be understood symbolically (remember the metaphor of God and His covenant people).

Out of all of the human relationships God chose to highlight in this book, He picked marriage. And not just marriage in general, but the pursuit and experience of sexual pleasure within marriage. The Song opens passionately with the bride pleading, "Let him kiss me with the kisses of his mouth—for your love is more delightful than wine."[6]

Because the Song uses veiled language, we often miss how erotic and sensual this little book of the Bible actually is. In *Intimacy Ignited,* the authors explain, "God inspired Solomon to use poetic imagery to portray explicit sexual acts. For example, when the husband enters his wife's 'garden,' the image refers to [her vagina]. 'Mandrakes' and 'pomegranates,' which spill forth their seed when opened, symbolize fertility and virility; 'honey' and 'wine' convey intense, erotic desire. Because all of the sexual references are cloaked in symbolism, a child could pick up the Bible, read the verses, and find no offense. But a husband and wife could understand the terminology and find specific sexual instruction."[7]

The Song of Solomon's veiled meaning is so explicit that modern translators toned down the message in some places. For example, in 5:14 the bride is praising her husband's naked body. It reads like this in the King James Version: "His body is an ivory panel bedecked with sapphires." You are probably picturing a six-pack based on that description. In the original Hebrew, it's more like this, "His abdomen is like a bright, sharp piece of ivory, wrapped like a jewel." Some commentators believe this is a veiled reference to the male genitalia in an aroused state.[8]

The Song of Solomon is an explicit declaration that God is all for sexual ecstasy. As imperfect as your marriage may be, He wants you to swim in the pleasure of becoming one. He created your mind with the capacity for imaginative and creative love making. The Song encourages husbands and wives to meditate on the beauty and eroticism of each other's bodies. God says to the couple, "Eat, friends, and drink; drink your fill of love."[9] He says this to you too!

Solomon uses similar language in his advice to young men in Proverbs 5:18–19. After warning them of the danger of sexual immorality, he writes,

> May your fountain be blessed,
>   and may you rejoice in the wife of your youth.
> A loving doe, a graceful deer—
>   may her breasts satisfy you always,
>   may you ever be intoxicated with her love.

To be "intoxicated" or drunk means that your whole being is overtaken by a substance so powerful that shortcuts your thinking. Solomon urges us to continually be drunk with the wine of sexual love. When was the last time you truly felt "intoxicated" with your spouse? If it's been a while, don't blame the Bible.

Look at the puzzle box.

Let's connect this principle back to our covenant with God. Have you ever met a sour Christian? Picture that man or woman who does everything God asks of them, but their lives have no joy. You probably don't have to work too hard to conjure up the image. Most movies and novels portray Christians in this light. All rules and duty, no fun.

Author and pastor Jim Cymbala tells the story of a woman he noticed as a child:

> In the little church I grew up in, there was a middle-aged woman who was always dressed in black. She wore a black dress, a black hat, and black shoes. She always sat alone with a tight, pursed look on her face, and she never talked to anyone. I never even saw her smile. She would enter into the meetings and pray and listen to the Word and then leave. As a young child, I was afraid to even get near her. She looked like she had been baptized in lemon juice!
>
> One day I got up the courage to ask another adult about her. "What's with that lady?" I asked.
>
> The man gave me an understanding nod as if he knew from experience something that I didn't. "Oh, her. You can tell she walks very close to God."
>
> My little mind struggled with the thought. *Walking close to God means you never smile? It means you have no friends? You never rejoice in Jesus?* Why would anyone want to get close to God if that's what it did to you?[10]

While being a Christian means at times experiencing hardship and choosing the more difficult road, it is meant to be a journey of joy. Jesus said, "I have come that they may have life, and have it to the full."[11] The apostle Peter wrote, "Though you have not seen him, you love him; and even though you do not see him now, you believe in him and are filled with an inexpressible and glorious joy."[12]

Walking closely with God should not make us austere and somber. Even if we measure our days with greater wisdom, knowing God gives us reason to rejoice at all times.[13] We learn to celebrate God's love for us even when life is difficult. Remembering and celebrating our covenant with God becomes part of our normal personal and church life.

The genuine Christian life is a life of passion. Just as with sex, our passion for God is guided and protected by the other pillars: faithfulness, intimate knowing, and sacrificial love. Our faith isn't driven by raw emotion, but unparalleled joy and passion should be the regular expression of knowing Him.

This joyful celebration with God, interestingly, impacts our brain in a way that is similar to sexual intimacy. Prayer and meditation increase dopamine and serotonin levels. Even secular scientists encourage people to pray and meditate because of the calming and healing effect it has on the body: "Prayer reduces the experience of anxiety, elevates a depressed mood, lowers blood pressure, stabilizes sleep patterns and impacts autonomic functions like digestion and breathing."[14] Similar to sex, singing releases the bonding hormone oxytocin. This is particularly true when we sing with other people.[15] And it turns out that when we dance, we get a powerful mixture of dopamine, oxytocin, serotonin, and endorphins.[16]

Neuroscientist Daniel Amen notes the connection between spiritual intimacy and sexual pleasure: "Both peak experiences seem to be processed primarily on the right side of the brain, especially the right temporal lobe and prefrontal cortex. So enhancing one experience may, in fact, help the other. Enhancing right-hemisphere function may enhance both religious and sexual experience."[17]

Unfortunately, many of us experience worship as reading words off a screen or watching the most talented people in church perform. The focus of the average church service is the preacher giving a message. While God's Word is central to knowing Him, it shouldn't necessarily be the highlight of our time together. We completely miss the fact that God is inviting us into a corporate celebration of pleasure as we worship Him together.

Being a Christ follower is an invitation to *enter into* praise, worship, regular celebration, and pleasure in God's presence. Your walk with the Lord needs to have regular times of both personal and church worship, just for the sake of intimacy and celebration. When you do this, you are more prepared to face the challenges that will inevitably come in life. You need this refilling time of spiritual intimacy with God, just as a husband and wife need the positive celebration of sexual intimacy.

ENTERING INTO PLEASURE

This past weekend, I was at a women's conference where three hundred and fifty of us spent an hour worshiping the Lord. After a few songs, I noticed I felt like an observer. Women around me were dancing, waving their hands, and singing to the Lord at the top of their lungs. I was singing, but as if on the periphery of the action. I'm a terrible dancer. I have no rhythm and even clap off beat (my husband will verify this). And so I held back. It's as if the Lord spoke to me, "Juli, worship is not a spectator sport. You have to enter in and lose yourself in the moment. Forget about your insecurities and just celebrate with Me."

Sex is much this same way. We must choose to *enter into* the pleasure of oneness, letting go of our inhibitions and insecurities. Your spouse can't do this for you. It's your choice. Here are a few specific ways you can choose to mature in your capacity to experience sexual pleasure together.

Learn your pleasure patterns.

Don't assume that just because you are a sexually active adult you know everything about sex. God created our bodies with great complexity. Even the most seasoned married couple has things to learn in general about sex and even more to learn about their own unique experience.

To begin with, read a book that explains the basics of sexual pleasure. *A Celebration of Sex* by Doug Rosenau is a great choice. You don't have to read all 380 pages. He has specific chapters on the erogenous zones, natural aphrodisiacs, sensual massage, creative intercourse, and male and female sexual responses. Cliff and Joyce Penner have also written Christian books like *The Gift of Sex* and *Get Your Sex Life Off to a Great Start*.

Then there are things about sexual pleasure that you can't read in a book but you can only discover for yourself. Sexual pleasure is a moving target. Hormones, age, stress, physical health, energy, emotional intimacy, and many other things all converge impacting your sex life and ability to experience pleasure.

Where do you like to have sex? What time of day? What helps you focus on each other and what distracts you from intimacy and pleasure? Where and how do you like to be touched? Sexual pleasure may be natural, but it's also something that needs to be cultivated.

You may be reading this book thinking, "I'm not sure I even have a pleasure pattern." I've talked to hundreds of women over the years who simply have no desire for sex. Female sexuality and pleasure patterns are complicated. A woman's sexual response will be impacted by hormone imbalances, a lack of emotional connection, body image, past trauma, fatigue, the need for control, and underlying beliefs that lead to sexual shame.

Guys, don't be surprised if your wife's orgasm is elusive or if she is difficult to arouse. Don't accept this as the status quo of your marriage and settle for one-sided pleasure. God created your wife to be complex, and He challenges you with learning about her sexuality. While she needs to take responsibility for her own sexual response, your wife also needs you to be part of that process.

If this describes your marriage, I recommend two books by Cliff and Joyce Penner: *Enjoy!: The Gift of Sexual Pleasure for Women* and *A Married Guy's Guide to Great Sex*. Read these books together as a guide to discovering her unique pleasure patterns. A helpful resource for wives is *Passion Pursuit,* a ten-week Bible study Linda Dillow and I wrote to help women embrace God's purpose for pleasure in intimacy. You might also consider reaching out to a pelvic floor therapist or Christian sex therapist.

For others, you need to learn new pleasure patterns as the brain may be connecting sexual touch with memories that sabotage oneness, either through the repeated use of pornography or the powerful impact of past trauma. That might be why you or your spouse can't experience sexual touch without your mind going to harmful places.

But there is good news! God made our brains to be elastic. This means that we can forge new pathways and let weeds grow over the destructive ones. Having sex the way you have always had it just reinforces fear, shame, or harmful fantasies, so you might need to temporarily abstain from sex for a season as you build healthy pleasure pathways. This will take hard work, and you may need the help of someone with specific training in sexual trauma or sexual addiction.

Know the boundaries.

In graduate school, I learned about a study that observed children's play patterns both with a fenced-in playground and open playground.

> On playgrounds without fences, the children tended to gather around the teacher, and were reluctant to stray far from her view. On playgrounds that were fenced in, however, they ran all around the entire playground, feeling more free to explore. The researchers concluded that with a boundary, in this case a fence, children felt more at ease to explore the space.[18]

I've found the same to be true for sex. Freedom comes through knowing where the fences are. Couples often ask, "What's okay for us to enjoy in the bedroom?" If you aren't sure if God is okay with oral sex, it's going to be difficult to fully enjoy it. But if you are one hundred percent convinced that God says, "Go for it!" you'll be much more likely to find pleasure there.

God has set up some clear "fences" around the playground of sexual pleasure. Some people get confused about whether what God said no to in the Old Testament still applies in our day. For example, is it okay to have sex during a woman's period since the Old Testament law said not to? The Old Testament emphasized being ceremonially pure as a physical way of distinguishing God's people from the rest of the world. Since Jesus paid the sacrifice for our sin, being ceremonially clean isn't an issue anymore. However, all of God's people are still called to be morally pure, and sexuality is a big piece of moral purity.

Moral purity means that sexual expression is reserved for the covenant of marriage between a husband and wife. God puts fences around your marriage to ensure that sex is between you and your spouse, not just in body but also in your mind and imagination. Within this "party for two" there is great freedom to have fun and explore.

God tells us to be wise and loving toward each other as we navigate our sexual freedom. The Bible doesn't give a definitive no to things such as sex toys or oral sex, and you'll find very different opinions from Christian leaders on all of these topics. When Paul was teaching the early church, they had a lot of questions about how to handle their Christian freedom. Rather than creating lists of right and wrong, Paul taught them to use discernment: "'I have the right to do anything,' you say—but not everything is beneficial. 'I have the right to do anything'—but not everything is constructive. No one should seek their own good, but the good of others."[19]

There are many things in your marriage that you are free to do and enjoy. When you are not sure whether something is okay, ask questions like, "Does this build love in our marriage? Is the focus only on us? Does it in any way harm my spouse? Do we both enjoy it? Does it help us grow as lovers?"

Ultimately, you have to seek God's wisdom for setting fences within your own marriage. If you and your spouse disagree on a "gray area," listen and learn to love each other through the decision. Figuring out boundaries together gives you great opportunities to seek the Lord's guidance and to learn how to love each other more deeply.

The other three pillars of faithfulness, intimate knowing, and sacrificial love make sexual pleasure safe to pursue. Brooke, who was in the pilot study for this book and shared her story earlier of recovering from pornography and the impact of an open marriage, expressed that she was afraid of pleasure within her marriage because pleasure brought so much destruction. "Then I realized that sexual pleasure is one-hundred percent safe if the other three pillars are there. Are we faithful to each other? Are we pursuing true intimacy? Are we unselfishly giving and receiving love? If the answer is yes, I know I'm safe to fully enjoy!"

Relearn how to play.

Playfulness is perhaps the greatest sign of freedom in your sexual relationship. Gary Thomas explains, "Our play makes a statement to the world; indeed, it is an act of witness. Far from being a distraction, it loudly proclaims that we, the guilty, have been declared innocent. We, the imprisoned, have been set free."[20] In this light, Christians should be the most playful lovers. As God sets you free from sin, shame and insecurity, the natural response should be unrestrained enjoyment! Doug Rosenau describes the importance and quality of playfulness in building sexual intimacy:

Playfulness is perhaps best described by the terms *joyful excitement, eager curiosity, lighthearted fun, and spontaneous frolicking.* Playfulness is about the ability to be unpretentious and candid as you demand things with enthusiasm and laughter—expecting your needs to be met. You cannot *work* at creating better love-making: you and your mate have to *play* at it.[21]

Be creative, try new things (in bed and out of bed), don't worry about making a mess, and be willing to laugh when things don't turn out the way you thought they would. If you need a little help, there are plenty of Christian books and websites that provide creative, romantic ways to have fun together. When Mike and I were once in a rut, we used our competitiveness to our advantage. We challenged each other to see who could be the most creative planning date night. He won by planning a "Mission Impossible" date that had me on a scavenger hunt until I ended up meeting him for a romantic dinner all alone in front of a fireplace.

Some of your attempts at adventures might end up as a fun memory to laugh together. Linda Dillow, who wrote the study *Passion Pursuit* with me, shared how she tried to get creative for her husband's birthday:

> I went to where our camper was stored and set it up for a party. Balloons, a cake, dinner all prepared plus fun snacks and, of course, gifts. When I did the setup, the weather was nice for January. Five hours later, it was snowing. So we trudged through snow to the camper, laughing, and had a sweet time of dinner, intimacy, and a party in a camper that wasn't exactly warm. So we left early still laughing about my attempt at creative passion in the snow![22]

Celebrate in every season.

Darcie and Joe are newlyweds, trying to figure out the awkward dance of sharing their bodies and hearts.

Justine and Julio are navigating the hopes and disappointment of trying to conceive. Sex feels more like a reproductive laboratory than a space of fun or love.

Pete and Hayley are flat-out exhausted chasing four boys around the house. They have no time to even think about sex.

Jack and Robyn are more concerned about the potential sex lives of their teenagers than their own. The ups and downs of parenting have kept them too busy to work on their own relationship.

For Bonny and Keith, the kids are finally gone, but so is their sex drive. When Bonny hit menopause, her body stopped responding.

You get the point. No matter how old you are, how long you've been married and what your backstory includes, you will never have the perfect conditions for sexual pleasure.

An old Italian proverb reportedly paraphrased by Voltaire says, "The perfect is the enemy of the good." This wisdom certainly rings true for sex. Something or someone gets in the way of pleasure, making you feel like you want to give up.

A nagging conflict is hanging over your head.

You can't climax when you want to.

You don't like the way your body looks or you aren't attracted to your spouse's body.

It's too early in the morning, too late at night, or in the middle of a busy day.

You can't concentrate.

You can't have intercourse because of a medical issue.

You're pregnant or you can't get pregnant.

You're out of work or you have too much work.

If you wait until conditions are just right to pursue pleasure, I promise you it will never happen. Great lovers make the most of whatever they have in any given situation. They find ways to compensate for what's lacking and lean into what's good.

There is always something to celebrate in your marriage. Even through the roughest of seasons, there is good. One couple described themselves in a "sexless marriage." Because of a combination of emotional and physical issues, they hadn't had intercourse in over a year. I asked them, "I know you can't have intercourse right now, but when was the last time you were sexual with each other?" They looked at each other puzzled. How could they be sexual without intercourse? There are so many ways this couple can sexually celebrate with each other even if intercourse isn't possible. They can touch and taste and talk and stimulate one another. They can appreciate what they love about each other's bodies and being naked with one another.

Some seasons of marriage will be filled with grief and hard work. But even in those seasons, don't forget to celebrate the small victories and find comfort in each other's embrace.

Francie and Wyatt, parents of six young children, describe how God met them as they intentionally chose to celebrate together through a grueling season of marriage:

Early in our marriage we started taking local mini getaways a few times a year, in order to connect deeply without the distractions and pressures of daily life. As our family and responsibilities grew, we realized that these intentional getaways were not just good ideas, but vital for growing our marriage.

Recently, we were in such a fragile place emotionally and physically, we knew we needed more than a night or two at a local hotel. So, we splurged and went to Florida for a week-long getaway. Each day that we were there, we made connection and intimacy our main focus. We could have seen this trip as an escape from "real life," with our beach novels and umbrella drinks as our priority, but we were drawn to a different place, a different pace, together.

We arrived feeling weak. We moved slowly. We rested to-gether. We connected in physically intimate ways in the morn-ing, and again in the afternoon. We were tender and attentive to each other throughout the day as we processed life, hardships, hopes, and fears. We took several beach walks, collected shells, and even painted on the porch each evening (though neither of us are artists by any stretch of the imagination!). By the third day of being intentionally intimate physically, we noticed something special happening. Our minds were clearer. Our hearts were more open. Our bodies were experiencing greater levels of desire and attunement to each other. Our emotions were more connected to each other. Our intimate times were gaining momentum with self-giving, mutual pleasure and deep joy. The darkness was lift-ing, and our hope was rising. God was healing our sorrow-filled, weary souls as we opened ourselves to each other and to Him, naked and unashamed. As we prioritized pleasure, intimacy, and oneness, we found streams of healing washing over us.

I am not saying that after this trip all our stress, sorrows, and health struggles disappeared. We are very much still work-ing through them. But, on that trip a new level of oneness was experienced; a oneness that is helping us lean into each other through the struggle. We continue to be amazed at the kindness and provision of our Creator, who gave us the gift of physical intimacy in marriage, for the good times and the hard times. The gift that can bring reprieve, hope, connection, oneness, and an intimate knowing of each other as our brains and bodies are flooded with powerful stress relieving endorphins and hormones. We were reminded again that married sex can be a powerful gift when shared in self-giving covenant love, and deeply rooted in trust; a gift that can impart soul healing and physical restoration in ways that we never knew possible.

Paul wrote, "Whatever is true, whatever is noble, whatever is right, whatever is pure, whatever is lovely, whatever is admirable—**if anything is excellent or praiseworthy**—think about such things."[23] Notice that he didn't write "if *everything* is excellent or praiseworthy." Even through the deep valleys of marriage and your sexual journey, there are good things to enjoy. Don't let what is lacking rob you of God's invitation for you to "Eat, friends; drink and drink deeply, lovers."[24]

Chapter 8

Take the Next Step

For ten years, Mike and I had the joy of living in Colorado Springs where I fell in love with mountains. Every day I stepped outside our house to see the looming majesty of Pike's Peak. I often found myself rearranging my schedule so I could carve out a few hours to hike or trail run in the foothills. Six times, I tackled the challenge of climbing Barr Trail, all the way to the top of Pike's Peak, a thirteen-mile, one-way journey with an elevation gain of 7,800 feet. In order to summit before the thunderstorms roll in, you have to start hiking around 4 a.m. Six hours later, my legs would be aching and my lungs desperate for oxygen in the thin air. Just taking the next step required will power. I'd remind myself, "You *chose* to do this. What were you thinking? Remember never to do this again." But once I reached the summit, I would be ready to sign up for the next climb. Every day, when I looked at Pike's Peak, I'd think, "I climbed that!"

Like hiking a mountain, your journey toward sexual wholeness can feel like a massive undertaking. Remember, even a thirteen-mile hike up a mountain is composed of small steps, one after the other. Some of the steps in the journey are effortless while others require incredible determination to keep going.

Throughout this book, you have learned that sexual intimacy

in your marriage is an earthly metaphor for God's covenant love. You've been challenged to grow in the four pillars of God's covenant love: faithfulness, intimate knowing, sacrificial giving, and passionate celebration. You've begun to realize how events from your past and long-held assumptions keep you from receiving God's love and offering it to your spouse. Hopefully, you now have a vision of where you want to go; but maybe you're not sure if you have the strength to get there. As you stand there in the middle of the trail, maybe you realize that you've come too far to turn back, but the road ahead just feels impossible. You're tired. You're discouraged. You're afraid to hope. Remember this . . .

It's a journey of faith.

The author of the book of Hebrews tells us that the only way we can please God with our lives is to be people who live by faith. Faith means living by truths and convictions that sometimes fly in the face of everything around us. Faith is putting confidence in what you hope for—walking as if what you believe actually is true. It takes faith to believe what you've read in this book: that sexuality and marriage are more than what the culture presents them to be, that Jesus' blood really does purify you from all sin and unrighteousness, and that God wants an intimate relationship with you. "Without faith it is impossible to please God, because anyone who comes to him must believe that he exists and that he rewards those who earnestly seek him."[1]

When you encounter difficult stretches of the journey, the only thing that may keep you going is faith—faith for what God can do in the middle of your mess today and faith in what He promises for your future.

In Hebrews 11, we read about ancient people who walked by faith—people like Noah, Abraham, Rahab, Sarah, and Samson. Notice that the people mentioned in this "cloud of witnesses" were very far from perfect. Along with their decision to live by faith, they also had times of doubt. Some of them made some terrible decisions along the way, but what set them apart was the determination to live by faith when it mattered most. Their lives give witnesses to God's faithfulness, not that He gives us everything we want here on earth. In fact, Hebrews says that these people died without seeing the complete answer to their prayers. Yet, they trusted beyond what their physical eyes could see. They put faith in what the metaphor of sex points to: God's faithful, eternal, and covenant love.

I can assure you that many men and women before you have walked this journey of faith. Some have struggled with the exact challenges, temptations, and disappointments that you are currently facing. They would tell you that the road has not been easy, but God is faithful to His promises.

Faith means taking the next step.

There are times when God asks us by faith to take a big step. More often, His redemption looks like consistent, small steps of obedience. Confess a sin. Delete an app. Be the first to apologize. Listen graciously. Reach out to a friend. Join a support group. Call a counselor. A faithful life is nothing short of the consistent practice of obeying God in the little things.

You might wish that God would ask you to make one big gesture of obedience rather than a series of minor daily sacrifices. Small steps toward wholeness take a long time, and you want instant relief. You want to see immediate change in your marriage or spouse. God could snap His fingers and bring instant healing, but He doesn't, so you wonder, *God, why don't You work faster?*

> **There are times when God asks us by faith to take a big step. More often, His redemption looks like consistent, small steps of obedience.**

God works in our waiting. The journey itself is the trial that produces patience, kindness, trust, mercy, and love. Are you waiting for your spouse to get on the same page as you? Are you waiting for the pain and triggers to go away? Do you wake up every morning wondering if today is the day you will finally experience freedom?

While you might wish for God to "zap" you and make all things well in a moment, the reality of walking in His truth is usually much more like an arduous hike up a mountain. Be patient with yourself. Be patient with your spouse. If you fall down, get back up. Proverbs reminds us that "though the righteous fall seven times, they rise again."[2]

Veronica describes that she isn't yet where she would like to be, but she also isn't where she once was:

When I was twelve years old, I found some porn videos in my dad's office and was curious. Unfortunately, my response wasn't repulsion or "gross" but rather curiosity that led to a porn addiction that I'm still battling today. To make things more complicated, I watched porn very early in our marriage (within the first few months), which I believe contributed to our sexless marriage (going on three years now). It wasn't until this past year that I finally got protection on all my devices. I know my porn addiction covers a plethora of trauma, abuse, and pain in my childhood, and I know it's like a leech in our marriage.

I now realize the damage years of pain, trauma, and shame have done to me mentally and emotionally. I read John 5:1–15 about the paralytic and how he suffered for thirty-eight years in pain holding on to his mat waiting to experience healing and freedom. For me, the mat represents my identity and how I have been holding on to shame, an unhealthy perspective of my identity, and the strongholds of my sex life.

A few weeks ago I was lying in bed and felt a heavy burden

for my addiction and thought patterns. I was so burdened I started to pray. In my prayer, the Lord was showing me that trying to earn His grace through my behavior wouldn't be enough to heal me. His grace was the only way. I cried so hard and realized that my trespasses and sins were no greater or lesser than others. That it takes such a gracious and loving heavenly Father to cover my shame! It is a long journey, but God is healing me.

Veronica is walking by faith. It doesn't take faith to believe what *feels* true. Faith is when we put our confidence in truths that are at times difficult to live by. Your journey toward sexual wholeness and freedom will require you to lean into faith in God, that He is good, that He is your Redeemer, and that He will be faithful to what He promises.

Your sexual journey is not about where you are going, but who you are becoming.

Most of us have a very limited capacity to wait, especially when we are uncomfortable. It takes faith to believe that God is working, even in our waiting. In Hebrews 12 and throughout the New Testament letters, we read that God uses long-term difficulties to develop godly character.

Your sex life matters because of the character it exposes and develops within you. What you have read in this book has challenged not only how you view sex, but how you will respond as a result. The most important thing about you is who you choose to become. Will you stay selfish or will you learn to love as Jesus loves? Will your heart remain hard or will you open yourself to healing and intimacy? Your sexual journey is not about where you are going, but who you are becoming.

FAITH IN GOD'S GOODNESS

Over the last few years, John 11 has become a very powerful passage in my life. This chapter of the Bible tells the familiar story of Jesus raising Lazarus from the dead.

Lazarus, Mary, and Martha were siblings, all close friends with Jesus. These three siblings provided a home where Jesus found love, rest, and companionship. The sisters sent the desperate message to their friend, Jesus, that their brother was very sick. Curiously, instead of traveling to be with Mary and Martha or healing Lazarus, Jesus stayed right where He was. He told His disciples, "This illness will not end in death. No, it is for God's glory so that God's Son may be glorified through it."[3]

Two days later, Lazarus died. Now Jesus wanted to go visit His friends. "Our friend Lazarus has fallen asleep; but I am going there to wake him up." His disciples are super confused by this. They said, "If he sleeps, he will get better." Jesus spoke plainly, "Lazarus is dead, and for your sake I am glad I was not there, so that you may believe."[4]

Jesus' words make sense to us today because we know the end of the story. But imagine being the disciples who didn't know that Jesus was going to raise the man from the dead. Jesus' words and actions made absolutely no sense. Why would He be glad that His friend died? The next scene adds to their confusion. Mary and Martha are torn with grief over their brother's death. They both say to Jesus, "If you had been here, my brother would not have died."[5] In other words, "Don't you love us? Why don't you care about our pain? Why did you do nothing and allow this horrible tragedy to happen?"

Have you ever felt that way? Have you wondered why God's mighty hand didn't move to save you from pain and loss?

Mary and Martha didn't understand Jesus' apparent inaction, but they knew He loved them. Even their friends and neighbors knew of Jesus' friendship and love for this family. There is an incredibly touching and emotional scene where Jesus expresses anger at death and weeps with His friends Mary and Martha. He hates seeing their pain, even knowing that it will soon be replaced by joy.

In the midst of this tension, Martha makes an astounding statement of faith, "Lord, if you had been here, my brother would not have died. But I know that even now God will give you whatever you ask."[6] Martha had faith in a victory even in the wake of such great loss.

There are aspects of your sexual journey that simply don't make sense. Why would God allow this beautiful metaphor to be so horribly destroyed in your life? Why does He continue to allow evil like abuse and exploitation? Why is the journey of healing so long? How can there be a victory in such pain?

Friend, you and I have not yet witnessed our resurrection. We are living in the tension of knowing God loves us, but wondering why He didn't act as we think love would dictate. By faith, we believe that someday we, like Mary and Martha, will see the unfolding of God's glory even in the ashes of our loss. But for now, we cling to His love and the assurance that God is angry at death and weeps with us in our grief. It takes faith to believe in a victory when all you see is defeat. Will you trust in God's love and goodness, waiting and praying for a resurrection that you can't yet see?

FAITH IN GOD'S REDEMPTION

The reality of the Christian life is one of constant surrender. As you grow in your relationship with God, you will run into places of your heart that seem paralyzed by fear or compromised by sin. This is also true on the journey of sexual intimacy. There may have been times while reading this book when you felt like you hit a wall. *I just can't do that.* Or *intellectually I know that's true, but I can't accept it as true for our marriage.* God redeems when He breathes life into what was once dead. He frees us from what once kept us in bondage. We have a part in this redemption as well. We have to invite God into the wounds and hidden places of our heart.

God won't redeem what you refuse to expose. This means that for God to work in your marriage, you may have to enter some pretty messy places. I've met many couples who long for freedom and true *yada*, but they stay in hiding because of the stink. There are marriages that are "quasi-healed" and have hit a plateau of intimacy because they are afraid to talk through the hard things. An affair is swept under the rug because it's too painful to acknowledge. You ignore an addiction because confronting it might be too disruptive. Or you limp along, allowing your past to haunt you, but refusing to invite God into the mess.

Before Jesus spoke life into Lazarus's body, He addressed the physical barrier of a sealed tomb. Instead of opening the tomb, He told the people who were mourning Lazarus's death to do it—"Take away the stone."[7]

The people didn't act right away because there was a very practical problem: the stink. Martha's first thought was of the smell of a man who has been dead for four days. In the King James translation, Martha simply says, "Lord, by this time he stinketh."[8] As you read this book, you might have the same fear. You want God to work but you're afraid it's going to stink.

When Martha raised this very practical concern, Jesus responded by saying, "Did I not tell you that if you believe, you will see the glory of God?"[9] He didn't promise her it wouldn't stink, but that the smell would be of little consequence compared to the beauty of the redemption they would witness. The same is true of you. It may be messy to roll away that stone, to be honest about your struggle and to revisit buried wounds. But the glory of God will far outweigh the disruption of inviting Him into your mess.

God doesn't insist that you roll away the stone that seals your pain. He invites, patiently waiting for you to respond, promising that He will speak His healing power into your life.

So many Christians have portions of their sex lives sealed behind a stone. They tell themselves, "The past is in the past." Their fear keeps them from inviting the resurrection power of God into the dark places of their hearts. While the past is the past, the enemy uses our wounds and memories of sin to keep us from true intimacy.

While your marriage battles threaten intimacy with your spouse, the spiritual battle threatens your intimacy with God.

A lot of talk about sex in the church is defensive—how to keep the bad stuff out. Remember that God is a God of offense. He not only teaches us to guard and defend our hearts, He also reclaims what has been lost.

Your sex life is not just an issue between you and your spouse. It is also a spiritual battle of freedom and bondage. While your marriage battles threaten intimacy with your spouse, the spiritual battle threatens your intimacy with God. You were made for fellowship with Him, and Satan will do anything he can to separate you from God. If you have experienced a deeper sense of God's love just through reading this book, that makes Satan furious! As you and your spouse heal together and learn to love with covenant love, the devil will do whatever he can to discourage and distract you. So, yes, there is a very real spiritual battle around your heart, your healing, and your marriage.

The spiritual battle for your sex life is less about what happened to you in the past and more about the lies the enemy planted in the pivotal moments of your life. Satan takes advantage of the events of our lives and sets up strongholds of fear and shame. An eleven-year-old sees porn for the first time and can't forget it. A six-year-old is inappropriately touched by a babysitter and lives with unspoken shame for decades. A teen's parents go through a brutal divorce after infidelity, and she still can't make sense of it in her forties and finds it hard to trust her husband.

Jesus said that Satan is a liar and that his native language is to tell us lies. Satan will always leave a "calling card" in the sealed-off areas of our lives . . . he will plant lies that feel more true than the truth. This is what ultimately keeps you in debt.

Lie: My wounds are so deep, they can never be redeemed.
Truth: Nothing is too difficult for the Lord.[10]

Lie: My sins are so great, I can never be fully cleaned.
Truth: "As far as the east is from the west, so far has he removed our transgressions from us."[11]

Lie: I can't be satisfied in my current marriage. I need more.
Truth: "My God will meet all your needs according to the riches of his glory in Christ Jesus."[12]

Lie: No one understands my pain. I'm all alone.
Truth: "The LORD is close to the brokenhearted and saves those who are crushed in spirit."[13]

Lie: I don't have what it takes to fight this battle another day.
Truth: "His divine power has given us everything we need for a godly life through our knowledge of him who called us by his own glory and goodness."[14]

Lie: I'm better off navigating my sex life the way I think it should be.

Truth: "The world and its desires pass away, but whoever does the will of God lives forever."[15]

Remember, your sex life has areas of strongholds, not simply because of what happened in the past, but because of the lies that have taken root as a result.

One couple I talked to described feeling stuck in their marriage several years after the husband had been unfaithful. They had been through intensive individual and marital counseling that helped them work through anger and forgiveness, but they didn't know how to re-engage sexually. I asked them to tell me more.

The man explained that he couldn't forgive himself. Sex would be too intimate and too much to ask for from his wife, given what he had done. His wife agreed. She couldn't imagine how they could begin to rebuild sexual intimacy. Although she believed her husband had grown and changed, she didn't want to risk being wounded again.

They were at an impasse. Where is the enemy in this couple's story? Yes, he was there prompting the infidelity, tempting this man to sin against God. But he's still at work keeping this couple bound by the past.

Through Christ, this couple would have an awesome victory if they experienced the full redemption of their marriage and sex life. How the enemy would be defeated in their story of freedom from bondage! But he still has them bound, in debt, to the betrayal of the past.

The enemy camps in the pain and tells you lies that eventually become your personal truth. These are strongholds. *I can't trust anyone. I can't let anyone get too close. If I trust, I'll always get hurt.* Lies lead to vows, promises we unconsciously make to ourselves. *I'll never be that vulnerable again.* Those lies represent strongholds in our hearts that keep us from intimacy with God.

There is a difference between accepting limitations and living by lies. While God doesn't promise to erase our past or remove our scars, He does promise to set us free from the spiritual bondage of them. It is absolutely critical for you to understand the difference. Some pain you will endure comes with living in a fallen world, but another kind of pain is rooted in fear and condemnation that you should absolutely refuse to continue living in. I don't know where the enemy has set up camp in your sexuality, but I do know that he doesn't belong there. He has no right to stay. Friend, it's time to roll away the stone so that you can be free.

Pursue truth.

If the broken areas of your heart contain strongholds of lies, then there is an obvious antidote. The truth. Every good friend, every helpful counselor, every healing tool will have the goal of helping you walk in truth. The truth about sex and marriage. The truth about your value. The truth about sin and forgiveness. The truth about your spouse. The truth about God.

Unfortunately, a lot of sources that claim to help us heal actually lead us away from truth. A good example of this is the way secular counselors and self-help books handle the topic of shame. Most will try to convince you that you can self-talk yourself out of shame: *I'm beautiful. I'm strong. I'm a good person. I am enough.*

This doesn't work. Do you know why? Because you intuitively know that some of your shame has aspects of truth. Your body is not perfect. You are not always beautiful or strong or good. You know that selfishness, lust, and evil lurk somewhere in the streams of your heart.

Psychological self-talk is ultimately based on faith in yourself. That will only get you so far because you know better than anyone how frail and sinful you actually are. But faith in God stakes your life on believing that God is who He says He is. Even when it doesn't feel true, you walk in the confidence that He will be faithful to what His covenant promises.

We are so blessed to have direct access to God's truth through the Bible. Unfortunately, the truths in God's Word go unmined by many Christians who ignore, reject, or modify the Bible. The Bible is offensive! No one wants to hear that we are hopeless and helpless without the saving power of Jesus Christ. We don't want anyone to shine a light on our selfishness, idolatry, bitterness, and self-righteousness. And so we settle for pleasant memes and watered-down devotionals that will tell us only what we want to hear.

I don't know about you, but I want a doctor to tell me the truth, not tickle my ears with empty assurances when I need serious medical intervention. God is the great Physician who will not spare your feelings at the expense of keeping you in bondage. God wants you to expose the truth about your sin, your pain, and your shame, but also about His love, grace, and mercy. God's Word tells us, "Faithful are the wounds of a friend, but deceitful are the kisses of an enemy."[16] You need sources of healing that are courageous enough to reveal truth, both the truths that feel like a healing balm and those that expose festering wounds.

Allow God's Word to be the "true north" of the compass of your life. Read it, study it, digest it. Measure your beliefs and experiences in light of it. But remember that God's truth becomes transformational when we connect it with *yada*. The Bible is not an end in itself, but the means through which you can personally know God.

Truth is a person, not an idea.

I often hear people say, "I know the truth in my head, but I don't yet believe it in my heart." Perhaps as you've learned truths through this book, they haven't yet transformed your thinking. You've thought the same way for so long that God's truth about sex feels distant, like a faraway country you hope to someday experience.

Let me ask you to consider a very personal question: Is your knowledge about God first-person, or are you simply banking on what someone has told you about God? It is not enough to live on secondhand truths about the Lord. The only knowledge powerful enough to defeat fear and shame is the *yada* of knowing God yourself. Someone else can't convince you that God loves you. You need to hear it from Him. Don't let me tell you there is nothing to fear, you need to hear from the almighty God, "Do not fear, for I am with you."[17] Truth isn't just a new way of thinking; it means embracing a person. Not only does Jesus *speak* the truth, He *is the Truth*. The most powerful truth is not just cognitive (in our heads) but relational (in our hearts). Only when we worship God and *yada* Him will the lies begin to feel untrue.

One of my favorite books is called *Secrets of the Secret Place* by Bob Sorge.[18] In this book, Bob explains that we nurture the presence and power of God in our lives by the daily habit of spending time alone with Him. Just like you have a time and a place to work on intimacy with your spouse, you commit to a time and a place to build intimacy with God.

If I could take everything I've learned—from an MA, MS, and doctorate in psychology; over twenty-five years in practical ministry; and all the hours I've spent counseling and boil them down to the one thing that will make the greatest difference in your life, it would be this: know Jesus. Cry out to Him. Run to Him. Worship Him. Say yes to Him. Reading the Bible, spending time in prayer, going to counseling, getting plugged into a discipleship group . . . these are not magic bullets that heal you, but pathways to knowing a Savior who will free your captive heart. The journey of freedom isn't primarily about having enough willpower and self-discipline, but comes through knowing Jesus.

THE COURAGE TO REACH OUT FOR HELP

Some of the most sacred moments of my life has been when someone shares with me a secret for the first time:

I had an abortion when I was seventeen.

I was sexually abused by my cousin.

I had an affair two years ago that I can't tell my husband about.

I've been faking orgasm my entire marriage.

It's one thing to name your pain or shame for yourself, but you put a stake in the ground when you share it with someone else. I have never met anyone who experienced significant sexual healing without someone else on the journey beside them. It's not enough to read in a book that God loves no matter what you've done or suffered through. It's a completely different experience to look someone in the eye as they show you God's grace, love, and compassion.

You were not meant to heal alone. You are not able to heal alone. You need God's help, and you also need to lean on the people He has placed around you. Unfortunately, your fear may be keeping you from the relational intimacy required for your healing. *What if I were honest with my spouse or counselor? What if they judge me or reject me? Maybe it's just safer to keep everything sealed in a tomb of silence.*

My friend Ginger shares from personal experience about her choice to reach out for help as a survival of horrific childhood abuse:

For me to start the healing process, I had to be willing to ask others for help. It required me to take the risk of reaching out and being vulnerable. There was nothing pleasant about telling someone how much of a mess my life was in. The rewards for taking that risk have been life changing.

There had to be a willingness to look at my pain, not ignore it, but choose to work through it. This was one of the hardest parts of my healing journey. It required me to take a leap of faith with God and with others. Was I willing to trust that God would meet me in my pain? Was I willing to trust that my counselor would know how to handle my pain with gentleness and empathy? Was I willing to believe that my pain would not destroy me? My answer was yes.

If you know the story of Lazarus, you know that the watching crowd did roll away the stone, and Lazarus walked out of the grave wrapped up like a mummy. Imagine witnessing this scene! While the people around were probably astonished and afraid, Jesus addressed the next very practical issue. Lazarus was alive, but he was still bound in the graveclothes. Instead of magically removing them or asking Lazarus to free himself, Jesus told the people, "Unwrap him. Set him free." Jesus spoke life. Lazarus walked out of the tomb. The people in the community helped set him free.

This man had been dead for four days. Not only did the graveclothes probably smell of decaying flesh, but they also would have made the people touching them ceremonially unclean. Jews were not supposed to touch anything that had contact with a dead body. And so they probably paused before approaching Lazarus. *Do we dare get dirty to set this man free?*

This physical event of resurrection is symbolic of the process God uses to bring freedom into the imprisoned or dead areas of your heart. You roll away the stone, God speaks life, and you have to be willing to let people enter into the messy places on the road to freedom.

Who is the community around you, helping you walk toward freedom? Ephesians 4 says that God gives His people different kinds of spiritual gifts so we can all grow in maturity, rooted in Christ's love. This means there are Christians around you who have the wisdom, knowledge, mercy, prayer support, and encouragement that you need as you journey toward wholeness. Yes, it will mean taking a risk to ask for help. Your friends, pastor, counselor, and mentors are imperfect people who may sometimes let you down and you will fail them as well. But you need healthy, grace-filled relationships to become a whole person.

FINAL THOUGHTS

The four pillars of covenant love—Faithfulness, Intimate Knowing, Sacrificial Love, and Passionate Celebration—are not meant to just be aspirational in your sex life but possible. Real-life people are walking the same journey you are. Just like people of faith mentioned in Hebrews, other Christians living today can give you hope for the work God wants to do in your heart and marriage. Throughout this book, you have read testimonies from real people with messy marriages who would tell you that God is faithful to His promises. Brooke, who you met earlier, is one of them:

> Dane and I celebrated our tenth anniversary this weekend (praise Jesus we can even say that!).
>
> We are living proof of the power of God's design for intimacy. Living proof that there is nothing so far gone (and goodness gracious were we so far gone!) or too damaged that God can't redeem and restore. We just didn't have any tools, any help, any guidance or support; once we had those, God stepped in and messed us all up in all the right ways. As He did that, and things got even messier for a while, we continued to have consistent support through the mentorships/friendships and tools that we found at Authentic Intimacy.[19]
>
> As we celebrated our anniversary, we spent hours reveling in the beauty of God's grace and redemption for our story. Not

just that we are simply "still married" but that we are actually experiencing LOVE growing in our hearts. Where there was once emptiness, anger, shame, unfaithfulness, resentment, confusion, pain, addictions, brokenness . . . there is grace, lightness, freedom/recovery, laughter, respect, love, clarity, faithfulness, security, and identity. We are amazed with the presence of our Creator. HE is the story we want to tell. He is the heartbeat of this marriage. He is the heartbeat of this story. We still have work to do (don't we all?) but there is so much hope now.

God is all about reclaiming the lost ground in our hearts and marriages. There is no marriage that is "too far gone" for His redemption. As Brooke shared, she and Dane are on a journey of redemption. They are committed to inviting the Lord to reclaim their marriage from past wounds, shame, fear, and brokenness. As they walk this faith journey together, they are free to give more and more of themselves to God and to one another. Couples like Brooke and Dane engage in this hard work because they recognize the importance of redemption.

Please understand that Satan's primary work *is not* ruining your sex life, but separating you from the life-giving love of God. Therefore, healing is not simply the ability to enjoy sex, but the freedom found in knowing you are intimately loved by God.

As we close, I want to remind you of something I wrote in the very beginning of this book: Sex will never be a neutral issue in your marriage, and sex will never be a neutral issue in your relationship with God. Sex cannot save you, nor can it destroy you. It is a physical expression of what happens in the deeper places of your heart. Friend, the journey of sexual wholeness in your heart and your marriage will include challenges and victories. It is worth the journey.

Now to him who is able to do immeasurably more than all we ask or imagine, according to his power that is at work within us, to him be glory in the church and in Christ Jesus throughout all generations, for ever and ever! Amen. (Eph. 3:20–21)

Discussion Guide

The words you read in *God, Sex, and Your Marriage* are intended to provide a biblical framework for you to think and talk about sexual intimacy within your marriage. This study guide can help you digest those concepts, both in your personal considerations as well as in discussion with your spouse.

I've broken the questions into a few separate sections, knowing that individuals and couples may be at different points in their journey.

Sharing your thoughts about the chapter: These questions are intended to give you some structure to talk through some of your basic thoughts, feelings, and questions coming out of the chapter.

Questions for personal reflection: These questions go a bit deeper. If you do not feel comfortable sharing at this level of discussion, consider these questions in your personal time with the Lord.

Discussion prompts for you as a couple: These questions help you take the content and put it into practice. You may run into a few questions or suggestions here that you don't feel quite ready for. That's okay!

Getting God's perspective: This section will provide one or more passages of Scripture for you to consider as you work through the material.

CHAPTER 1
KNOWING YOUR BACKSTORY

Sharing your thoughts about the chapter:

1. What is your biggest takeaway from this chapter?

2. What emotions did this chapter evoke for you?

3. What lingering questions do you have after reading this chapter?

Questions for personal reflection:

1. *You don't come to your marriage bed with a blank slate. You come with expectations, fears, secrets, shame, and an unspoken understanding of what "good sex" should look like.* What do you think about this statement?

2. List a few ways in which the culture's story of sex has impacted how you think about sex within your marriage.

3. What do you think about this statement?: *The culture's greatest fault is not that it overpromises on sex but that it underpromises.*

4. What did you learn about sex from the church, Christian parents, and other religious sources of information?

5. List a few ways in which the church's story of sex has impacted how you think about sex within your marriage.

Discussion prompts for you as a couple:

Take some time to share about your backstory of sex. Take turns sharing and listening.

1. How did you learn about sex as a child and teenager?

2. What role have the wrong "stories of sex" had on how you currently think about your sex life?

Pray together that God will help you to learn His perspective of sex in your marriage.

Getting God's perspective:
Read Romans 11:33–12:2.

1. What do these verses say about God's ways?

2. What does verse 11:36 teach about the purpose of God's creation? How would you apply this to His creation of sexual intimacy?

3. What does God call us to do in response to His greatness and goodness?

4. How does 12:2 instruct us to surrender our backstory to God's truth?

CHAPTER 2
GOD'S STORY OF SEX

Sharing your thoughts about the chapter:

1. What is your biggest takeaway from this chapter?

2. What emotions did this chapter evoke for you?

3. What lingering questions do you have after reading this chapter?

Questions for personal reflection:

1. Based on what you read in this chapter, how would you explain the role between sex and covenant in your marriage?

2. Why do you think God's enemy, Satan, chooses to so aggressively attack sexuality?

3. What are three ways you have personally experienced spiritual attack in your sex life?

Discussion prompts for you as a couple:

1. How is covenant love different from every other kind of love?

2. How does what you've read about covenant love challenge how you approach sex in your marriage?

3. How does understanding God's story of sex give you hope for sexual intimacy within your marriage?

Pray together, inviting God to reclaim the story of sex in your marriage.

Getting God's perspective:

Read Ephesians 5:21–33.

1. Read Genesis 2:21-25. How does Paul connect the "first wedding" in Genesis to the last wedding of Christ and His bride?

2. Why do you think this is called a mystery? How is that mystery being revealed to you in your marriage?

3. What does the real-life work of becoming "one flesh" teach you about Christ's love for us?

CHAPTER 3
WHOLENESS BEYOND SEXUAL PURITY

Sharing your thoughts about the chapter:
1. What is your biggest takeaway from this chapter?

2. What emotions did this chapter evoke for you?

3. What lingering questions do you have after reading this chapter?

Questions for personal reflection:
1. How has purity culture impacted your view of God and sex?

2. How would you describe the difference between sexual purity and sexual integrity? Which one is more difficult?

3. To what extent is God a part of your sex life? Where do you have invisible "Do not enter" signs that need to be torn down?

Discussion prompts for you as a couple:
1. What do you think it means to grow in sexual integrity or maturity?

2. How might your sex life look different a year from now if you committed to growing in sexual integrity?

3. What is one thing God is showing you about what it means to surrender your sexuality to Him?

Pray together, thanking God that He is able to forgive your sin and make you pure. Ask Him to give you a vision for what it looks like to grow in sexual maturity.

Getting God's perspective:

Read 1 Corinthians 6:9–20 and 2 Corinthians 5:14–17.

1. How does your identity in Christ change the way you view your sexual past? Your spouse's sexual past?

2. How does your identity in Christ change the way you view your sexual choices today?

CHAPTER 4
PILLAR 1—FAITHFULNESS

Sharing your thoughts about the chapter:

1. What is your biggest takeaway from this chapter?

2. What emotions did this chapter evoke for you?

3. What lingering questions do you have after reading this chapter?

Questions for personal reflection:

1. Why is faithfulness foundational to building every other aspect of sexual intimacy?

2. Why is healthy jealousy a good thing within a marriage covenant? How would you define the difference between healthy and unhealthy jealousy?

3. What emotional needs might you have attached to sex, making it feel more like a basic need?

Discussion prompts for you as a couple:

1. What do you think of the concept of "holy jealousy"?

2. Share your thoughts about this statement: *The most important ingredient of sexual intimacy is character.* Do you agree with it? Why or why not?

3. What role does discipleship and community play in how God wants to develop the character trait of faithfulness in your life and marriage?

Spend time thanking God for His faithfulness to you and asking for His help as you build and pursue faithfulness in your relationship.

Getting God's perspective:

Read James 4:1–12.

1. How does this passage describe unhealthy jealousy—the kind that causes divisions?

2. How does this passage describe God's holy jealousy?

3. What advice does this passage give about how to deal with our past sin and current temptations?

CHAPTER 5
PILLAR 2—INTIMATE KNOWING

Sharing your thoughts about the chapter:

1. What is your biggest takeaway from this chapter?

2. What emotions did this chapter evoke for you?

3. What lingering questions do you have after reading this chapter?

Questions for personal reflection:

1. How would you describe the difference between sexual activity and sexual intimacy?

2. How has your "activity" in trying to please God kept you from intimacy with Him?

3. Why is there "no such thing as risk-free *yada*"? What would you have to risk in order to pursue deeper intimacy with your spouse?

4. What are some ways that you have learned to hide your flaws and insecurities with people? How does this play out in your marriage?

Discussion prompts for you as a couple:

1. Talk about a challenge you are currently facing in your sex life. How might that challenge be an invitation to intimacy and vulnerability?

2. Look over the questions and activities suggested on pages 100–102. Choose one set of questions or one activity to engage in together this week.

Getting God's perspective:
1. Read Psalm 139, noticing all of the places the psalmist mentions *yada*. How is the relationship with God David describes a call to intimacy?
2. Read 1 Corinthians 13:4–7. How does this passage set the stage for intimacy in your marriage?

CHAPTER 6
PILLAR 3—SACRIFICIAL LOVE

Sharing your thoughts about the chapter:

1. What is your biggest takeaway from this chapter?

2. What emotions did this chapter evoke for you?

3. What lingering questions do you have after reading this chapter?

Questions for personal reflection:

1. Have you ever considered that self-control and self-denial are also part of marital sex? Why or why not?

2. Why is it important to remember that sacrificial love still has boundaries? How do we see this in the example of Jesus' life?

3. How do your limitations keep you from being a willing and cheerful giver in your sexual relationship?

4. When your spouse offers sexual love, which are you more like—the person who receives with gratitude or the one who complains or pouts because of what is lacking?

Discussion prompts for you as a couple:

1. Do you think traditional teaching on sex put too much emphasis on sexual rights and duties? Why or why not?

2. What does it look like to "nurture" the sex life of your spouse? How is that different than just having sex?

Getting God's perspective:

Read 1 Corinthians 7:1–6. Now read 1 Corinthians 13:1–7.

These passages are within the same letter written by Paul. How do they together teach you about what it means to love each other sexually?

CHAPTER 7
PILLAR 4—PASSIONATE CELEBRATION

Sharing your thoughts about the chapter:
1. What is your biggest takeaway from this chapter?

2. What emotions did this chapter evoke for you?

3. What lingering questions do you have after reading this chapter?

Questions for personal reflection:
1. What do you think of the idea of sex being the regular celebration of your covenant?

2. Why are the other three pillars of covenant important guardrails to sexual pleasure?

3. Why is it important to be confident in the boundaries of healthy, holy sexuality? How have undefined boundaries kept you from pleasure in your marriage?

4. How do the disappointments in your sex life keep you from enjoying and celebrating what is good during this current season of marriage?

Discussion prompts for you as a couple:
1. What are some barriers you face in enjoying sexual pleasure?

2. What can you do to address those barriers together?

3. What is one way you can "play" together this week?

Getting God's perspective:

Read Matthew 7:9–11.

1. Do you see God as a Father who gives good gifts to His children?

2. Do you believe that sexual pleasure in your marriage is a good gift from God? Why or why not?

CHAPTER 8
TAKE THE NEXT STEP

Sharing your thoughts about the chapter:

1. What is your biggest takeaway from this chapter?

2. What emotions did this chapter evoke for you?

3. What lingering questions do you have after reading this chapter?

Questions for personal reflection:

1. What have you read in this book that will take faith to believe?

2. In what ways has your sexual journey caused you to question the love or goodness of God?

3. "The spiritual battle for your sex life is less about what happened to you in the past and more about the lies the enemy planted in the pivotal moments of your life." List some of the lies Satan has planted in your life related to intimacy and sexuality.

4. What truths have you learned in this book that expose those lies?

Discussion prompts for you as a couple:

1. What would it look like for us to "roll away the stone" and invite God to speak life into the wounded places of our marriage?

2. How have we seen God's power at work in our lives already?

3. Who are the people God has placed in your life to help you "remove the graveclothes" of your brokenness?

Spend some time in prayer, thanking God for how He is working in your hearts and marriage and asking Him to give you faith to continue to trust Him in this journey.

Getting God's perspective:
Read John 11:1–44.

1. Why do you think Jesus was angry and cried even though He knew Lazarus would soon be resurrected?

2. Why do you think Jesus raised Lazarus from the dead?

3. How does this miracle give you faith in the work God wants to do in your heart and marriage?

Resources

JULI SLATTERY'S MINISTRY

Authentic Intimacy, authenticintimacy.com
Java with Juli Podcast, javawithjuli.com
Finding the Hero in Your Husband: Embracing Your Power in Marriage,
Dr. Juli Slattery
Rethinking Sexuality: God's Design and Why It Matters, Dr. Juli Slattery
Passion Pursuit: What Kind of Love Are You Making? Linda Dillow
and Dr. Juli Slattery

SEX IN MARRIAGE

Intimacy Ignited: Discover the Fun and Freedom of God-Centered Sex,
Dr. Joseph and Linda Dillow and Peter and Lorraine Pintus
A Celebration of Sex: A Guide to Enjoying God's Gift of Sexual Intimacy,
Dr. Doug Rosenau
Married Sex: A Christian Couple's Guide to Reimagining Your Love Life,
Gary Thomas and Debra Fileta
A Celebration of Sex After 50, Dr. Doug Rosenau
A Celebration of Sex for Newlyweds, Dr. Doug Rosenau

RESOURCES FOR WOMEN

Jennifer Degler Ministries, jenniferdegler.com
Passion Pursuit: What Kind of Love Are You Making?, Linda Dillow
and Dr. Juli Slattery
Enjoy!: The Gift of Sexual Pleasure for Women, Joyce and Clifford
Penner

RESOURCES FOR MEN

Be Broken Ministries, bebroken.org
The Married Guy's Guide to Great Sex, Clifford and Joyce Penner

CHRISTIAN SEX THERAPISTS

sexualwholeness.com
mycounselor.online
passionatecommitment.com
Focus on the Family's Christian Counselors Network,
focusonthefamily.com

TRAUMA RECOVERY

Restoring the Pleasure, Clifford and Joyce Penner
*The Wounded Heart: The Heartache of Sexual Abuse and the Hope of
Transformation*, Dan Allender
Understanding Sexual Abuse, Tim Hein
When the Woman You Love Was Abused, Dawn Scott Jones
When the Man You Love Was Abused, Cecil Murphey

PORNOGRAPHY, SEXUAL ADDICTION, AND AFFAIR RECOVERY

Be Broken Ministries, bebroken.org

Pure Desire Ministries, puredesire.org

Restored2More.com

Hope Quest, hopequestgroup.org

IITAP (specialized therapy for sexual addiction), iitap.com

No Stones: Women Redeemed from Sexual Addiction, Marnie Ferree

Healing the Wounds of Sexual Addiction, Dr. Mark Laaser

Fight for Love, Rosie Makinney, fightforloveministries.org

Unwanted: How Sexual Brokenness Reveals Our Way to Healing, Jay Stringer

The Anatomy of an Affair: How Affairs, Attractions, and Addictions Develop, and How to Guard Your Marriage Against Them, Dave Carder

Hope after Betrayal: When Sexual Addiction Invades Your Marriage, Meg Wilson

Acknowledgments

I'm grateful to partner with the outstanding publishing team at Moody Publishers, specifically Judy Dunagan, Amanda Cleary Eastep, Melissa Zaldivar, and Connor Sterchi. Thank you also to Robert Wolgemuth and Andrew Wolgemuth for your help in getting this book published.

Kristi Miller, thank you for your help as an initial editor and Julia Mitchell for helping me with research. Hope Francis, Joy Skarka, Suzanne Dubois, and Jacci Roberts, it takes a committed team to accomplish this work of reclaiming God's design for sexuality. I couldn't do it without you! Ginger, Marie, Carrie, Bonny, and Abby, thank you for your faithfulness in prayer.

Michael Sytsma, I am so grateful for your expert review of this manuscript. Cory and Keyla Morgan and Pete and Cheryl Henderson, thank you for bravely leading the first group of couples through the pilot studies.

On a personal note, thank you to Mike, my husband and best friend, who has helped me write this book through the journey of our twenty-eight years together.

Notes

Chapter 1: Knowing Your Backstory

1. This is a common paraphrase of Blaise Pascal's statement: "What is it then that this desire and this inability proclaim to us, but that there was once in man a true happiness of which there now remain to him only the mark and empty trace, which he in vain tries to fill from all his surroundings, seeking from things absent the help he does not obtain in things present? But these are all inadequate, because the infinite abyss can only be filled by an infinite and immutable object, that is to say, only by God Himself." Blaise Pascal, *Pensées*, trans. W. F. Trotter (New York: Random House, 1941), 134–35.

2. "What Americans Believe about Sex," Barna Group, January 14, 2016, https://www.barna.com/research/what-americans-believe-about-sex.

3. Mary Ann Watson and Randyl Smith, "Positive Porn: Educational, Medical, and Clinical Uses," *American Journal of Sexuality Education*, 7 (April 2012): 122–45, https://www.researchgate.net/publication/254356638_Positive_Porn_Educational_Medical_and_Clinical_Uses.

4. Quote attributed to Don Shrader. As cited in *Blackie's Dictionary of Quotations* (Mumbai: Blackie & Son, 2008), 249.

5. Augustine, *The Soliloquies of St. Augustine*, trans. by Rose Elizabeth Cleveland (Boston: Little Brown, and Company, 1910), 29, https://oll-resources.s3.us-east-2.amazonaws.com/oll3/store/titles/1153/0579_Bk.pdf.

6. From "The Estate of Marriage," *Luther's Works*, vol. 45 (Fortress Press), trans. by Walther I. Brandt. As cited at https://pages.uoregon.edu/dluebke/Reformations441/LutherMarriage.htm.

7. Quote attributed to Peter Lombard, "Behavior: Sex Talk Through the Ages," *Time*, January 9, 2004, http://content.time.com/time/subscriber/article/0,33009,993155,00.html.

8. Ruth Smythers, "Instruction and Advice for the Young Bride," *The Madison Institute Newsletter* (New York: Spiritual Guidance Press, fall 1894).

9. 1 Timothy 1:15.

10. Psalm 119:105.

Chapter 2: God's Story of Sex

1. Friedrich Nietzsche, *Twilight of the Idols*, trans. by Richard Polt (Indianapolis, IN: Hacking Publishing Company, Inc., 1997), 6.

2. Juli Slattery, *Finding the Hero in Your Husband, Revisited: Embracing Your Power in Marriage* (Deerfield Beach, FL: HCI, 2021), 165.

3. Genesis 2:24 NASB.

4. Ephesians 5:32.

5. Slattery, *Finding the Hero in Your Husband, Revisited*, 165.

6. *Java with Juli* (podcast), Episode #313, "The Greatest Love Story," June 1, 2020.

7. Matthew 5:6; Psalm 63:1; Isaiah 55:1; John 4:13–14.

8. Romans 8:15; 9:26; Galatians 3:26.

9. Adapted from Juli Slattery's *Finding the Hero in Your Husband, Revisited*, 167.

10. Timothy Keller, *Preaching: Communicating Faith in an Age of Skepticism* (New York: Penguin, 2015), 104.

11. Hebrews 9:15.

12. "Moral Issues," GALLUP, https://news.gallup.com/poll/1681/moral-issues .aspx.

13. Timothy Keller, "Love and Lust," Sermon delivered May 6, 2002 at Redeemer Presbyterian Church, New York, NY.

14. Christopher West, *Theology of the Body for Beginners: A Basic Introduction to Pope John Paul II's Sexual Revolution* (West Chester, PA: Ascension, 2004), 12.

Chapter 3: Wholeness Beyond Sexual Purity

1. See 1 Corinthians 6:18; 10:8; 2 Timothy 2:22; 1 Thessalonians 4:3–5.

2. Hebrews 12:14; 1 Peter 1:16.

3. Ephesians 2:8–9.

4. 1 Corinthians 6:19b–20.

5. Nahum 1:7.

6. Deuteronomy 6:5; Matthew 22:37.

7. Howard Taylor, *Hudson Taylor's Spiritual Secret* (London: China Inland Mission, 1932), 229.

8. Genesis 2:25.

9. See Deuteronomy 31:6 and Hebrews 13:5–6.

10. "Worship," https://www.biblegateway.com/resources/dictionary-of-bible-themes/8629-worship-times.

11. Ecclesiastes 7:2.

12. Matthew 22:30.

13. C. S. Lewis, *The Four Loves* (New York: Harcourt, Brace, 1960), 6.

14. See 1 Corinthians 7:25–36.

Chapter 4: Pillar 1—Faithfulness

1. Matthew 22:37.

2. Matthew 10:37.

3. Timothy Keller, *Counterfeit Gods: The Empty Promises of Money, Sex, and Power, and the Only Hope That Matters* (New York: Penguin Random House, 2016), 31.

4. Mark Leary, "PEA, Oxytocin, and other Chemicals of Passionate Love," The Great Courses Daily, November 25, 2020, https://www.thegreatcoursesdaily.com/pea-oxytocin-and-other-chemicals-of-passionate-love/.

5. Daniel Amen, *Sex on the Brain: 12 Lessons to Enhance Your Love Life* (New York: Harmony Books, 2007), 65.

6. Ibid., 63–64.

7. Fight the New Drug, "4 Studies that Show How Porn-Obsessed Brains Can Heal Over Time," March 27, 2018, https://healingforthesoul.org/2018/03/4-studies-that-show-how-porn-obsessed-brains-can-heal-over-time.

8. Matthew 5:31–32.

9. Ephesians 4:15.

10. Gary Thomas, "The Only Woman in the World," August 27, 2015, https://garythomas.com/2015/08/27/theonlywomanintheworld.

Chapter 5: Pillar 2—Intimate Knowing

1. Genesis 4:1.

2. "Shakab," Bible Study Tools, https://www.biblestudytools.com/lexicons/hebrew/nas/shakab.html.

3. Exodus 33:13.

4. Doug Rosenau, "The Meaning of Lovemaking," session worksheet. Quoted by permission.

5. Ibid.

6. Cliff and Joyce Penner, "Formula for Intimacy" (handout), AACC lecture, September 2021, Orlando, Florida.

Chapter 6: Pillar 3—Sacrificial Love

1. Juli Slattery, *Finding the Hero in Your Husband, Revisited: Embracing Your Power in Marriage* (Deerfield Beach, FL: HCI, 2021), 172–73.

2. Walt Larimore and Barb Larimore, *His Brain, Her Brain: How Divinely Designed Differences Can Straighten Your Marriage*, (Grand Rapids: Zondervan, 2008), 111.

3. Preston Sprinkle, *People to Be Loved: Why Homosexuality Is Not Just an Issue* (Grand Rapids: Zondervan, 2015), 32.

4. Matthew 22:37–38.

5. Parts of this section were adapted from "Are You Entitled to (Good) Sex in Marriage?," Authentic Intimacy, November 18, 2020, https://www.authentic intimacy.com/resources/25140/are-you-entitled-to-good-sex-in-marriage.

6. See 1 Corinthians 13:4–8.

7. *The Gift of Love*, directed by Don Chaffey, 20th Century Fox, 1978.

8. Excerpt, 1 Corinthians 7:5–7 MSG.

9. See John 12:1–8.

10. See Luke 8:1–3.

11. See Matthew 21:1–9.

12. See Matthew 26:36–46.

13. See Matthew 26:36–46.

14. Douglas E. Rosenau, *A Celebration of Sex: A Guide to Enjoying God's Gift of Sexual Intimacy* (Nashville: Thomas Nelson, 2002), 5–6.

15. Juli Slattery, interview with Gary Thomas, *Java with Juli* (podcast), September 20, 2021, https://www.authenticintimacy.com/resources/35002/379-is-your-love-life-all-that-you-want-it-to-be?source=blog.

16. Luke 21:1–4.

Chapter 7: Pillar 4—Passionate Celebration

1. Gary Thomas, *Pure Pleasure: Why Do Christians Feel So Bad about Feeling Good?* (Grand Rapids: Zondervan, 2009), 36.

2. Timothy Keller, "Love and Lust," sermon delivered May 6, 2002 at Redeemer Presbyterian Church, New York, NY.

3. Juli Slattery, Interview with Michael Sytsma, *Java with Juli* (podcast), October 29, 2021.

4. Kristine Thomason, "10 Things You Never Knew about the Clitoris," Health, October 5, 2015, https://www.health.com/mind-body/10-things-you-never-knew-about-the-clitoris.

5. Proverbs 5:19.

6. Song of Solomon 1:2.

7. Joseph and Linda Dillow, Peter and Lorraine Pintus, *Intimacy Ignited: Discover the Fun and Freedom of God-Centered Sex* (Colorado Springs, CO: NavPress, 2004), xvii.

8. "Song of Songs 5," Bible.org, Bible Lessons International, 2012, https://bible.org/book/export/html/21127.

9. Song of Solomon 5:1 NASB.

10. Jim Cymbala, *Spirit Rising: Tapping into the Power of the Holy Spirit* (Grand Rapids: Zondervan, 2012), 77.

11. John 10:10.

12. 1 Peter 1:8.

13. See 1 Thessalonians 5:16–18.

14. Michael J. Formica, "The Science, Psychology, and Metaphysics of Prayer," *Psychology Today,* July 28, 2010, https://psychologytoday.com/us/blog/enlightened-living/201007/the-science-psychology-and-metaphysics-prayer.

15. "Why Sing Together? 1: Neuroscience and the Creator's Intentions," *Church Music* (blog), https://churchmusicblog.wordpress.com/2009/11/21/why-sing-together-1-neuroscience-and-the-creators-intentions.

16. "Dance for Your DOSE of Happiness and Health," Greater Good Science Center, https://www.daybreaker.com/wp-content/uploads/2019/03/DOSE-Greater-Good-Science-Center_Dance-For-your-DOSE-of-Happiness-and-Health.pdf.

17. Daniel Amen, *Sex on the Brain: 12 Lessons to Enhance Your Love Life* (New York: Harmony Books, 2007), 143.

18. Ibid.

19. 1 Corinthians 10:23–24.

20. Gary Thomas, *Pure Pleasure,* 73.

21. Douglas E. Rosenau, *A Celebration of Sex: A Guide to Enjoying God's Gift of Sexual Intimacy* (Nashville: Thomas Nelson, 2002), 13.

22. Linda Dillow and Juli Slattery, *Passion Pursuit: What Kind of Love Are You Making?* (Chicago: Moody Publishers, 2013), 174.

23. Philippians 4:8.

24. Song of Solomon 5:1 NASB.

Chapter 8: Take the Next Step

1. Hebrews 11:6.
2. Proverbs 24:16.
3. John 11:4.
4. John 11:11–12, 14.
5. John 11:21 and 32.
6. John 11:21–22.
7. John 11:39.
8. John 11:39 KJV.
9. John 11:40.
10. Jeremiah 32:27.
11. Psalm 103:12.
12. Philippians 4:19.
13. Psalm 34:18.
14. 2 Peter 1:3.
15. 1 John 2:17.
16. Proverbs 27:6 NASB.
17. Isaiah 41:10.
18. Bob Sorge, *Secrets of the Secret Place: Keys to Igniting Your Personal Time with God* (Grandview, MO: Oasis House, 2001).
19. Authentic Intimacy is Juli Slattery's ministry.

Java with Juli
WITH DR. JULI SLATTERY

The "Java with Juli" podcast features fresh, relevant and gospel-centered conversations about our sexuality. Dr. Juli Slattery dives into the "taboo" questions you're afraid to ask—or don't know who to ask—about intimacy, marriage, singleness, sexual addiction, and more. Every episode is an invitation to a biblical look at the good, the hard, the healing, and the holy in God's design for sexuality. Available wherever you get your podcasts. To learn more, visit AuthenticIntimacy.com.

A BIBLE STUDY FOR WOMEN ABOUT SEX?!?
NOW, *THAT'S* DIFFERENT!

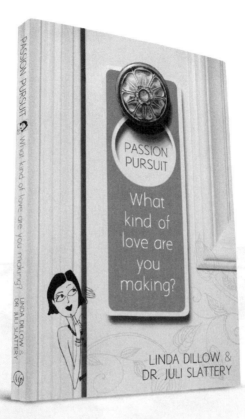

Can sex be holy *and* erotic? Does God have an opinion about sex? What's okay in the bedroom? This audaciously bold ten-week study will answer these and many other questions that women have but haven't had a trusted source for honest, biblical answers. Now they do.

978-0-8024-0639-2 | also available as an eBook

MOODY
Publishers®

From the Word to Life®

The **Healer** is inviting you...

Surprised by the Healer speaks comfort and courage to women who feel broken beyond repair. Weaving together Scripture, their own insights, and stories covering an array of painful experiences, the authors invite you to know the God who heals and to find your wholeness in Him.

978-0-8024-1340-6 | also available as an eBook

MOODY
Publishers®

From the Word to Life®